Friesens Corporation (PRINTER)
and the
Afton Historical Society Press (PUBLISHER)
are pleased to provide you with this
complimentary copy of

Patricia Condon Johnston's
New Book

Pie in the Sky
A Memoir About Writing and Publishing

Patricia Johnston is available for speaking engagements
and booksignings at bookstores, libraries, literary
events, writers' and publishers' conferences, art and
history events, rotary clubs, women's clubs,
professional meetings, and corporate events.

To schedule an appearance by Patricia contact:

Afton Historical Society Press
P.O. Box 100
Afton, Minnesota 55001
USA
1-800-436-8443 (Toll Free in the USA)
651-436-8443
651-436-7354 (Facsimile)

www.aftonpress.com

Friesens Corporation has been Afton's exclusive
printer for the last four years and we are tremendously
impressed with and indebted to them for their superior
quality and service. We highly recommend them to you.

To contact Friesens for information about
their printing services, to receive a quotation,
or to visit their facilities contact:

Friesens Corporation
One Printers Way
Altona, Manitoba, Canada
R0G 0B0
204-324-6401
204-324-1333 (Facsimile)

www.Friesens.com

BY PATRICIA CONDON JOHNSTON

Stillwater: Minnesota's Birthplace

Eastman Johnson's Lake Superior Indians

Minnesota's Irish

Pretty Red Wing: Historic River Town

The Minnesota Christmas Book

Minnesota: Portrait of the Land and Its People

Reflections: The White Bear Yacht Club, 1889-1989

MacGhillemhaoil, Volumes 1 and 2
(with W. Duncan MacMillan)

The Shape of Things: The Art of Francis Lee Jaques

Seth Eastman: A Portfolio of North American Indians
(with Sarah E. Boehme and Christian F. Feest)

MacMillan: The American Grain Family
(with W. Duncan MacMillan)

Pie in the Sky

Pie in the Sky

A Memoir About Writing and Publishing

Patricia Condon Johnston

Afton Historical Society Press
Afton, Minnesota

Frontispiece: Patricia Condon Johnston with Joe Demko, John Whitehead, Robert Hutchins, and Steven Heitzeg, Emmy Awards Ceremony, October 21, 2000

Designed by Mary Susan Oleson
with production assistance from Barbara J. Arney and Annie Klas

Note: Photographs with "tabbed corners" indicate family snapshots. Studio and historic photographs and other illustrations have square corners.

Library of Congress Cataloging-in-Publication Data

Johnston, Patricia Condon.
    Pie in the Sky: a memoir about writing and publishing / Patricia Condon Johnston. -- 1st ed.
        p. cm.

    ISBN 1-890434-38-8 -- ISBN 1-890434-39-6 (pbk.)
    1. Johnston, Patricia Condon. 2. Publishers and publishing--Minnesota--Biography. 3. Historians--Minnesota--Biography. 4. Afton Historical Society Press--History. I. Title.

Z473 .J77 2001
070.5'092--dc21   00-068992

Printed and bound in Canada

The Afton Historical Society Press publishes
exceptional books on regional subjects.

W. Duncan MacMillan   Patricia Condon Johnston
President   Publisher

Afton Historical Society Press
P.O. Box 100 Afton, MN 55001
1-800-436-8443
aftonpress@aftonpress.com
www.aftonpress.com

for Duncan MacMillan
with heartfelt thanks
for his many kindnesses
to me and my family

Contents

	Preface	xi
ONE	The Dodgers Dood It	1
TWO	Cereal Ads and Cider	26
THREE	A Mummy Dressed in Moccasins	49
FOUR	Fitzgerald Fever	68
FIVE	Minnesota's Earliest Whoopee-Town	85
SIX	College Made Easy	107
SEVEN	MacGhillemhaoil	125
EIGHT	No Middle Ground	155
NINE	The Coen Brothers' Mother	175
TEN	New York, New York!	195
ELEVEN	The Year of the Dragon	217
	Appendix AHSP Books and Awards	244
	Photo and Illustration Credits	248

Preface

I AM WRITING this book in the hope that it will inspire others to indulge in the joys of writing for publication. Writing is an immensely satisfying activity and one that has given tremendous focus to my life. In a sense, it has become my life. It is who I am. I am a writer. In the past twenty-some years, I have written hundreds of articles for dozens of magazines, ranging from *Americana, American History, Minnesota Monthly,* and *Twin Cities* to *Sporting Classics* and *Wildlife Art News,* as well as twelve books. Most, but not all, of my articles and books concern some aspect of American art or history.

Taking writing one step further, I am also now a publisher. I began by self-publishing and marketing my own books on Minnesota subjects in the early 1980s, five of them, one after another, beginning with *Stillwater: Minnesota's Birthplace* and concluding with *The Minnesota Christmas Book.* Today I have what I consider to be the best job in the world: I am the publisher at the Afton Historical Society Press in Afton, Minnesota.

Afton publishes beautiful and scholarly books on regional subjects that we market throughout the Midwest and, in some cases, nationally and even internationally. We are currently developing and publishing six to eight respectable books each year, each one of which makes us feel very good about what we are doing. We are also extending the reach of our publishing program with museum exhibitions and public television documentaries.

This book is the story of my personal journey in writing and publishing. I conceived of it as a "how to" in the form of a memoir. It is not a "how to write" book per se, because I don't believe that anyone can really teach another person how to write. What I can do, however, is tell you what has worked for me. I was lucky enough, for instance, to sell the first magazine article I wrote. A lot more than luck was involved, of course, and I have since written and sold enough articles to recognize what it was that I did right the first time.

I am thankful beyond words to have creative work that often literally consumes me. My writing and publishing duties provide the kind of never-ending challenge that I enjoy waking up to each morning. My work has made the good times in my life infinitely better and the terrible times bearable. It has opened up new worlds and experiences to me, and it can do so for you.

If you want to become a writer, and are willing to work relentlessly toward that goal, you will become one. The "willing to work" part is the key. I am not somebody special. I was a housewife and mother in my mid-thirties when I began writing. If I could do it, so can you. Whatever your age, if you want to write, I urge you to follow your heart. You have nothing to lose. Instead you might just wind up as happy and satisfied as I am to be a writer.

My first and most important advice to you is this:

Follow your passion and live your dream!

Pie in the Sky

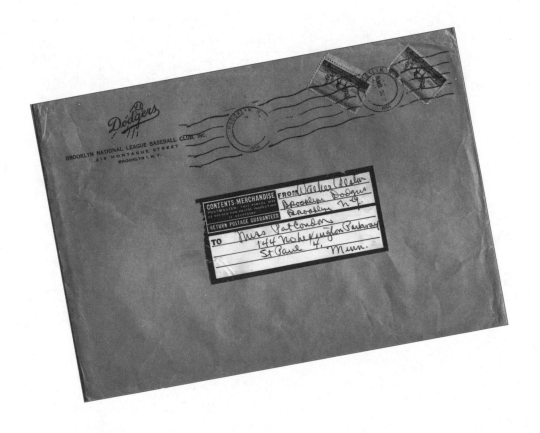

1

The Dodgers Dood It

LITTLE DID I REALIZE when I wrote my first magazine article more than twenty years ago that I was embarking on the adventure of my life. The opportunities for a free-lance writer to go places and meet people are virtually limitless. For one early assignment for *Collector Editions* magazine, my husband, Charlie, and I drove to Washington, D.C., where we visited with Walter Mondale's wife, Joan, about the modern art she was hanging in the Vice President's residence. Charlie did the driving and took the photos for the piece. Joan was promoting contemporary living American artists in this way and had enlisted the help of Smithsonian and other museum personnel who actually borrowed and installed the always spectacular artwork each year.

Another time, when we wanted to vacation in Ireland, Charlie and I collaborated on a travel article for *Twin Cities* magazine. Most of that trip was as idyllic as you would expect a trip to Ireland to be, until I asked Charlie to stop the car and take photos of the bunkers at a border crossing into northern Ireland. That got us surrounded by young British soldiers with their weapons drawn who wanted his film, which he refused to give up, and which, after determining that we were mere tourists, they finally let him keep.

Or there was the time, on one of our first trips to the Southwest (where we now have a small house), when we covered the opening of an exhibition of George Montgomery's western sculptures at Fenn Galleries in Santa Fe.

George had been married to Dinah Shore, and we chatted with him and his Hollywood friends. I shared my hors d'oeuvres that evening with singer Ed Ames. Charlie took my picture with comedian Jonathan Winters.

The fact that I was a writer for magazines gave me credibility, and I worked very hard at presenting myself well. On a

Jonathan Winters and me, 1977

trip to Denver to interview western art collectors Bill and Dorothy Harmsen for one of my first articles for *Americana* magazine, while Charlie drove, I read *How to Talk with Practically Anybody About Practically Anything* by Barbara Walters. By the time we reached Denver, I felt, quoting the dustjacket, ready "to talk with ease to tycoons, celebrities, VIPs, bosses, dates, men, women, children, old people, babies, you name it." Despite its 1970 copyright, this is still a wonderfully informative and entertaining book that I recommend for anyone who is in any way intimidated by meeting new people—which is most of us.

Magazine writing can lead a free-lancer almost anywhere. In my case, in addition to romantic locales and fascinating people, it led to writing books. It was a natural progression really. A time simply came when I wanted to expand on an article I had written for *Twin Cities* magazine. The result was *Stillwater: Minnesota's Birthplace*, a book that is still selling well many years later. Other magazine articles developed into additional books. Besides the books that I have self-published, I have also written books on assignment for other publishers.

That I pretty much fell into a wonderful life of writing still amazes me. I don't remember having any desire to write in my youth. Unlike F. Scott Fitzgerald, who grew up a few blocks away from me a generation earlier in St. Paul, I didn't spend my preteen years writing plays for neighborhood children to perform. By the time Scott was ten, he was keeping a "character book," in which he recorded his impressions of his playmates. There was little question that he intended to grow up to be a writer. Having shared his Summit Hill neighborhood and his Irish Catholic heritage, I've come to feel some connection to Fitzgerald—who was infinitely more fascinating than the characters he wrote about—but not because I ever hoped to emulate him.

I had a different dream. I wanted to be a country music singer. From the time I was five, I would listen enthralled to Eddie Arnold on the radio. A few years later, I was lip-synching the words to country music records in front of my bedroom mirror, practicing for when I grew up to be a star. I took piano lessons from the time I was in fourth grade and fantasized, too, of becoming a concert pianist or playing ragtime in a piano bar. Any thoughts of a career as a singer or piano player were doomed from the onset, however, by my fear of performing in public. I dreaded the annual piano recital, when I would invariably forget portions of whatever piece I had memorized. In time I learned to take to my bed, sick, on recital day, to avoid performing.

A generation later, my daughter Mary Sue Englund,

who suffers not a whit from stage fright, *did* grow up to be a country music singer, with her own band, no less. Every so often I'm able to spend a few days with her in Nashville, where, when she's not touring, she performs at the Wild Horse Saloon. Her success astounds and delights me. Now I am able to live out the country music dream vicariously through her, leaving me free to do my writing.

My baptism day, with my parents, Don and Betty Condon

I was my parents' first child, born in Minneapolis in 1939, when they were living on the second floor of my Condon grandparents' white frame duplex on Cedar Avenue. I remember especially the long side porch on the south side of the house that opened onto Grandma's sweet-smelling flower gardens. Grandma Anne Condon was a small, quiet-spoken, hardworking woman of German descent who had raised nine children through thin times and was spending her declining years caring for her invalid husband. Grandpa Condon had broken his hip several years before I was born and remained bedridden for the rest of his life, more than fifteen years.

The streetcars ran all day and night on Cedar Avenue, and I loved their clatter and rattle. One time, Grandma Condon was hit by a streetcar while she was crossing the street and landed in the "cowcatcher" grille on the front of it. After she got up and dusted herself off, Grandma apologized to the streetcar man for being in his way. That's the kind of person she was.

Grandma Condon and me

When I was three, and already had a younger sister, Colleen, and a brother, Tom, we moved to Duluth, where my father opened an office for Minnesota Blue Cross. We lived in three different houses in five years, the first two of them rentals, all of them large and lovely. My father was developing a passion for nice houses and would own several in his lifetime. Our third house was a large stucco-and-timbers house he purchased on East Third Street. I started second grade two blocks away at Holy Rosary Catholic School, where our nuns were Dominicans in white habits. Every chance I got, I played at playing tennis at the tennis club across the alley behind our house.

Our neighbors in Duluth included Pulitzer Prize-winning author Sinclair Lewis, who lived in an elegant cut-stone and brick house around the corner. Lewis liked to write on the brick patio in front of his house, so he had had the front steps walled up to prevent his

Tom, Dad, me, and Colleen

being interrupted by the mailman, leaving the only entrance to his house in the rear. One year I attended a Halloween party for neighborhood children on the third floor of Lewis's house, but this may have been after the author had moved on to Massachusetts. I don't remember him being there. I only remember bobbing for apples in a round tin tub, which I didn't find to be much fun.

When I was eight, my father was promoted to vice president of Minnesota Blue Cross, and we moved to St. Paul, where the insurance company had its headquarters in a three-story brick building on the corner of University and Raymond Avenues. My father had gone on ahead of us and purchased a three-story brick and stucco-and-timbers house at 144 North Lexington Parkway, within walking distance of St. Luke's Church and School. My mother hired a workman, a relative by marriage, to redecorate this house, top to bottom, as she always did with all of our houses. My father hired gardeners to landscape the front and back yards and plant flower gardens. In the dining room of this house, behind a hinged piece of dark oak paneling, was a secret compartment where the previous owner, a physician, had stored drugs. I used to stash small sums of money, mostly change, in this cubby.

The Lexington Parkway of my childhood was a gracious street of large, turn-of-the-century homes and wide boulevards. Two rows of stately elms formed a leafy arch over the roadway. Even while we still lived there, however, the city began widening the street, and the trees later fell victim to Dutch elm disease, so that the Lexington Parkway of today presents a rather barren vista. The large house we lived in has been converted to a group home for mentally challenged adults.

I was the oldest of six children and treasure my memories of growing up in that house. My sister Colleen and I shared two rooms on the third floor, which was our personal haven. We used one room for our bedroom, and the other was our playroom, although I don't remember playing much as a child. I always thought of myself as a young adult and tried to act like one. Colleen was ten-and-a-half months younger than me and rambunctious and high-spirited, while I prided myself on being "ladylike." I'm sure she had a lot more fun than I did. She used to crawl out one

of our third-floor windows to sun-
bathe on our steep roof in the summer—something I never would have
done for fear of falling off.

Each school-day morning, we
Condon children walked the four
blocks down Lexington Parkway to
St. Luke's Grade School. (Four of us
were in grade school in the late
1940s—me, Colleen, Tom, and Mary
Ellen, all of us born within the space
of four years.) The nuns were black-
robed Sisters of St. Joseph, and some
of these nuns could be very stern,
but they were good-hearted women
who had devoted their lives to serving
God and humanity.

Me and Colleen

School was easy for me, and I liked it and got good
grades. I thought I had some talent as an artist. One year I
drew large posters of saints to decorate our classroom. Some
days I helped in the school office, answering the phone and
running the mimeograph machine. After school, I joined a
Brownie troop that met in a basement classroom. Later, I
was a Girl Scout and earned dozens of merit badges (which
I think my mother still has someplace).

Summertimes, while my siblings spent a lot of time
outside playing what I considered "childish" games with
other children in the neighborhood, I was often inside with
a book. I loved to read and read everything I could get my
hands on, including my mother's selections from the Literary
Guild. Once or twice a week, I would ride my maroon-and-
white Schwinn bicycle to the nearest branch library at
Webster Grade School, about a mile away, to return books

and borrow new ones. I won contests for reading the most library books during the summer.

On my way to the library

The year I was seven I devoured Nancy Drew stories, and for decades, an engrossing mystery remained my favorite bedtime reading. I also loved the fairy tales of the brothers Grimm. I'm convinced that if you want to write, you must read, and read widely. I now also read a great deal of non-fiction, particularly American art and history subjects. My idol is historian Doris Kearns Goodwin, who won a Pulitzer Prize in history for her *New York Times* best-seller about the Franklin Roosevelts, *No Ordinary Time.* Her most recent best-seller is a memoir about growing up in the suburbs of New York in the 1950s, *Wait Till Next Year,* a book that also depicts a glorious era in baseball, one of my own passions as a girl.

My interest in history was kindled at St. Joseph's Academy for girls, where I attended high school. St. Joe's was about two miles toward downtown St. Paul from where we lived, and my dad drove me to school every morning, even though he worked in the opposite direction. I had carfare, ten cents, to take the bus home in the afternoon, but I usually walked with friends and spent my dime for a Coke at a drugstore on the way.

St. Joe's was the city's oldest school, founded by the Sisters of St. Joseph in pioneer St. Paul in 1851. I didn't especially enjoy the history classes at St. Joe's, which, as I recall, were fairly dry, but I was impressed with the history of the school itself and the nuns.

The Sisters of St. Joseph, who were mainly teachers and nurses, originated in France, where at least two of them lost their heads for their faith during the French Revolution. In 1836, at the request of the first bishop of St. Louis, six of these French nuns came to the United States and established a mother house at Carondelet, Missouri. Their expedition was financed by the Countess de la Rochejaquelin, who had sold her jewels on learning of the great need for missions among the Indians and white settlers in America.

Fifteen years later, four sisters of St. Joseph from Carondelet traveled up the Mississippi River to Minnesota Territory to open a school in the log church that had been St. Paul's first cathedral. The ragtag community that greeted them was a small village of frame and log huts containing something over a thousand souls, mainly half-blood Indians and French-Canadians with a sprinkling of Irish and Swiss. One of the sisters' pupils that first year in 1851 was Mary Mehegan, who would become the wife of railroad baron James J. Hill. During a cholera epidemic a few years later, the sisters turned the log building into a temporary hospital.

In 1863, on St. Anthony Hill, the sisters built the hand-some three-and-a-half-story yellow limestone building, now a National Historic Site, where I attended classes. Originally on the outskirts of the city, St. Joe's in those early days was a boarding school. Except for Sunday walks with the sisters, the students saw little of the outside world. According to an early handbook, each young woman was expected to pro-vide herself with black aprons, two veils, sewing materials, a silver goblet, and postage stamps. The dress code speci-fied: "For summer, a black dress with white waist; hat or bonnet trimmed with white. For winter, a black dress and cloak; hat or bonnet trimmed with crimson."

In my day, St. Joe's was no longer on the edge of the city. It had, in fact, been surrounded by urban blight (which has since been cleared and the area redeveloped). It was also no longer a boarding school, but we still wore uniforms—forest-green wool gabardine jumpers over long-sleeved white blouses with French cuffs and a green SJA monogram on the lapel. My mother ironed a fresh blouse for me every night, along with clothes for all the other members of the family. She even sprinkled and ironed my dad's boxer shorts.

Our green SJA jumpers were outrageously unfashionable. The top consisted of two halves that were loose and floppy (providing a convenient repository for carrying snacks to classes—which, of course, was forbidden, but which, of course, some girls did anyway). The pleated skirts fit snugly around our hips—more snugly on some than on others, depending on a girl's girth. If the sisters were after modesty, these jumpers didn't do it.

During my freshman year, the uniform included sturdy brown oxford shoes with nylon stockings (which, in an era before pantyhose, required a garter belt or panty girdle to hold them up). The next year the oxfords were out, and the new uniform shoes were all-green saddle shoes worn with white anklets and nylon stockings! The sisters must have thought the green shoes—which were outlandishly ugly—and anklets were somehow more stylish, but they also didn't want girls coming to school with *bare* legs. So we wore the anklets over our nylons.

In addition to the usual high school classes (which for me included religion, algebra, French, history, English, and music), my father insisted that I take typing and shorthand. He wanted to be sure that I would always be able to earn my own living, if necessary, as a secretary. Typing and shorthand are also helpful skills for a writer. With modern recorders, shorthand is not nearly as necessary as it once was, but I still use it on occasion because I prefer transcribing from shorthand notes over fiddling with a machine. It has something to do with my incompatibility with machines of any kind. (If I so much as try to use the copy machine in our office, it usually jams.)

My favorite class at St. Joe's was journalism. I was coeditor of the school newspaper, the *SJA Journal,* and I enjoyed every part of determining the paper's content, writing articles for it, and laying out the pages. I wrote a regular column that I had wanted to call "The Disposal" (garbage disposals being rather new at the time), but our adviser, Sister Isabella, thought that "Pat's Paragon" was a better choice, so "Pat's Paragon" it was. In the only issue I still have of the *Journal,* I have given over most of my column to a letter to the editor. This letter was apparently elicited by an earlier column of mine concerning the so-called "Loyal Order of Philogynistic Misogamists"—a fraternity for women-haters that supposedly existed at the College of St. Thomas in St. Paul.

> Dear Miss Condon [it began]:
>
> As one of your faithful and erstwhile silent readers (and admirers) it behooves me not to write a critical analysis of your column (gripe).
>
> However in the course of human events, when a libelous columnist like yourself sees fit to cut the tires of the only united and self-initiated club on the St. Thomas campus, then "war" becomes the epitome of action.
>
> Your description of we bachelors as "cowards" had dire effects on our membership. Since last Friday, our number has dwindled from 1378 merry women haters to we three. Besides Tommy Manville and King Farouk there is only myself. At our monthly meeting last night, we entertained ourselves by making paper dolls out of your column and sticking pins in your

pix. (Fun, eh?) Then we passed a resolution that henceforth our clique should be known only as the Hermit Club.

Now see what you have done, Lady Godiva.

Jack Kiesner
Ed.-in-chief of the
St. Thomas *Aquin*

I was sixteen at the time and tickled to be acknowledged by a college man, but my short stint as an editor on the *Journal* marked the extent of my writing career for the next twenty years. I'm reminded by Jack's letter that he and I dated once or twice. Then I began receiving calls from a friend of his, another "Tommy," as the boys at St. Thomas were called, who wanted to go out with me. This young man was from a prominent Minneapolis family, but we never got together. Shortly after I began hearing from him, he was sentenced to a term in the St. Paul workhouse for providing phony driver's license IDs to his underage friends. Many years later, I read in a Twin Cities newspaper that this failed forger had been named president of several area banks.

The only example of writing from my high school years that I still have is my junior term paper. I saved it for sentimental reasons, but I'm told that it now has some monetary value. It may be worth quite a lot, in fact, but certainly not because I wrote it. In a way, this term paper resulted from a trip that our family took during the winter of 1956 to Sanibel Island. My dad drove his big Buick Roadmaster with room for all of us, and it was a four-day trip to south Florida on mostly two-lane roads. Sanibel was a subtropical paradise waiting to be discovered, accessible only by ferry. Its tourist accommodations amounted to a handful of rental cabins and one small restaurant. Nowadays, whenever any mention of this trip comes up in our family, someone is bound to chirp, "Do you remember the sea urchins!" And we all do.

Sanibel had some of the best shelling in the world. My mother loved walking along the beach in the mornings, collecting shells deposited by incoming tides. We all did. One day, following a storm, Mom collected buckets of beautiful little round purple sea urchins. They really were irresistible, and for the next week or so, the sea urchins remained outside on the back porch of our cottage. When it came time for us to start back to Minnesota, she packed them in the trunk of our car.

By the second day on the road, the sea urchins were threatening to overpower us. "What is that smell?" complained first one child, then another, as the increasing stench from the dead and dying innards of these small shells infiltrated the car. My

On Sanibel Island with my sisters and grandmother: Mary Ellen, Colleen, Nana (my mother's mother), me, and O'Ann

mother pretended she couldn't smell them. She didn't want to give them up. My dad *could* smell them, however, and he finally stopped the car. One of us took a photo of my mother unloading cartons of sea urchins into a dumpster at a Dairy Queen, somewhere in Georgia.

Today my sister Colleen lives on Sanibel and owns a shell shop. Condominiums line the beach, and the island is reached by a bridge from the mainland. Colleen gets most of her shells from the Philippines.

While we were in Florida, my classmates wrote their junior term papers for English class. I had to write mine when we returned. We were supposed to have our subject matter approved by the instructor before proceeding with the paper, but I skipped this step. I had a great topic in mind, and I didn't want to take a chance on it being turned down. My title was "The 1955 World Series." In the history of major league baseball, this was the most exciting contest ever!

After winning the National League pennant the previous fall for the seventh time, the Brooklyn Dodgers were once again pitted against their perennial opponents, the New York Yankees. The Dodgers had *never* won a World Series, while the Yankees had won the last five in a row.

The 1955 series started out in Yankee Stadium with the Yankees winning the first two games, surprising no one. Then the contest moved to Ebbets Field, where the Dodgers won the next three games. Back in Yankee Stadium, the Dodgers' luck reverted, and Yankee southpaw Whitey Ford hurled a four-hitter against the Brooklyn team for a 5-1 win. The World Series was tied 3-3, and the next and final game would decide the winners. Quoting from my term paper:

> For the finale, October 4, in Yankee Stadium, Brooklyn manager Walter Alston sent Johnny Podres to the mound against Yankee hurler Tommy Byrne. Podres . . . casually remarked before game time, "I'll shut them out. I can beat those guys seven days a week." . . . Podres lived up to his prediction; although he put ten men on base he allowed not one to score. . . .
>
> Precisely at 3:43, the Dodgers scored the final put-out against the Yankees when Pee Wee Reese threw Elston Howard out at first. . . . 64,000 fans were on hand to cheer their victory which meant $8,595 for each of the [Dodger players].
>
> The Dodgers stormed in from the field like a tribe of Indians on the warpath, hugging and kissing everyone in sight. Within moments, the dressing room was swarming with

reporters, policemen, cameramen, and Dodgers. Broadcasters, anxious for an exclusive, shoved mikes in front of the weary players, but everyone was too excited to talk sensibly. . . . Don Newcombe and Duke Snider poured beer in each other's hats and then put them on for . . . photographers. . . .

Outside, all fury had broken loose in the streets of Flatbush. . . . "Dodgers Dood It," cried the *New York Daily Mirror*. According to the *Minneapolis Tribune*: "Nobody went home to supper. Nobody talked any sense. Everyone walked around with a goofy expression on his pan. For the unbelievable, the incredible, the impossible had come to pass: them Dodgers had put them Yankees under the stadium sod and now they was champions of the whole world."

I loved writing about the Dodgers. I loved baseball. While we were in Florida, my dad had taken us to see the St. Paul Saints in training at Vero Beach. The Saints were the Dodgers' triple-A farm club. Some of the Saints players moved up to Brooklyn, and Brooklyn sent others on their way down from the bigtime to St. Paul. Two or three of the Saints players lived across the street from us on Lexington each summer in rented rooms. My mother felt sorry for these young men, away from their homes, and invited them to Sunday dinner at our house. They gave Colleen and me free passes to the home games at Lexington Park, which was about a mile away on University Avenue, a good stretch of the legs on warm summer nights. Colleen started a fan club and collected autographed baseballs that she suspended by strings from the ceiling over her bed. I was always afraid that one of these balls was going to let loose one night and knock her out.

My term paper turned out great, I thought. I was proud of the research I had done at the downtown St. Paul Public Library, mostly in newspapers, and my snappy style of writing. So it came as quite a letdown when my English teacher was less enthusiastic. My topic was an inappropriate one, she said, and she gave me a C (leaving me to ponder the possibility that had I written about sea urchins, I might have earned an A?).

I wasn't at all sorry that I had written about the Dodgers, however. The first thing I did was to retype the title page to get rid of the offensive C; then I mailed it off to Brooklyn, asking the Dodgers if they would all autograph it. Which they did. I still have that term paper, in the same brown envelope in which manager Walt Alston returned it to me, signed by Jackie Robinson, Jim Gilliam, Carl Turillo, Duke Snider, Pee Wee Reese, Sandy Koufax, Roy Campanello, Carl Erskine, Ransom Jackson, Sal Maglie, Don Newcombe, Gino Cimoli, Gil Hodges—twenty-three Dodgers in all, five of them Hall of Famers. Walt Alston himself addressed the envelope with the Dodgers insignia on it; the postage stamps on it are two three-centers depicting a Charlie Russell painting of an antelope. I wouldn't part with this term paper for any amount of money, but I'm hoping it will one day get me on *Antiques Roadshow.*

The only other writing assignment I remember from high school was an essay that my senior year English teacher asked me to write for a national William Butler Yeats contest. I didn't know very much about the Irish poet, but I got a few books from the library. I remember sitting on my bedroom floor with them spread out around me and writing the essay there on the floor by hand, before typing the final draft on a small portable typewriter. I also remember my surprise when my essay placed third in the county competition, then second in the state, and, finally, fourth in the nation. How that progression was possible, I can't fathom, since the girl who placed first in the county lost out at the state level. But I have never since put much stock in contests.

*My term paper, autographed by the
1955 World Champion Brooklyn Dodgers*

Looking back, it becomes obvious to me that I enjoyed writing as a teen, and I am puzzled that I never considered a career in journalism. Young women in Catholic schools in those days seemed to have only three career choices: You could become a teacher or a nurse, and in either case you might also decide to enter the convent, or you got married and raised children. I actually toyed long and hard with the idea of becoming a nun. Two of my dad's sisters were nuns, and one of them in particular encouraged my vocation. But I liked boys too much to ever enter the convent.

My dream in high school consisted of a husband and a house and lots of happy children. My parents hoped that I would go to college, of course, but I couldn't see the point of it. I wanted to get on with the life I had envisioned for myself. By my senior year, I already had a husband picked out.

Charlie and me, December 28, 1957

I was sixteen the summer I met Charlie at our neighborhood drugstore on Selby Avenue, a block and a half from our house on Lexington Parkway. I had stopped by for a quick hot dog before catching a Selby-Lake bus to Minneapolis for my piano lesson at MacPhail Academy. Fresh out of the army, Charlie was having a Coke with an army buddy. Charlie's buddy was a neighbor of mine and introduced us.

Six months after graduating from
St. Joseph's Academy, I married Charlie
in a Christmas-week ceremony at St.
Luke's Church. My dad had made a
deal with me. If *Charlie* would go to college, he would give us his blessing. So
Charlie, who had spent two years in the
army in Korea, was just starting a four-
year course at the Minneapolis School of
Art (now the Minneapolis College of Art
and Design).

It was a gorgeous wedding, with
the huge church all decked out for
Christmas. My six bridesmaids wore
green velvet dresses and carried white
fur muffs with sprigs of holly. Two little

With D. J.

flower girls—my sister O'Ann and Char-
lie's sister Joyce—wore red velvet. Following the wedding
Mass, the photographer posed Charlie and me in front of the
Christmas manger scene. In another wedding photo, a family snapshot, I am holding my eighteen-month-old brother,
D. J., on my lap. (D. J. was named Donald John after my
father, who was also known as D. J.) I adored my small
brother and couldn't wait to have babies of my own.

Our first daughter, Patty, came into the world the following November. By then my father had purchased a home
large enough to accommodate all of us on Lake Harriet in
Minneapolis. Charlie and I lived on the third floor, where a
round turret room served as Patty's nursery. Our third-floor
quarters also had a wonderful rooftop deck, where I sometimes sunned myself in the afternoons. I had gone to work
right out of high school as a secretary for three cardiologists
in St. Paul, but after Patty was born, I switched to working

for a temp agency, so that my hours were more flexible.

My mother watched Patty along with D. J. while I was at work. Then our son Charles was born, and D. J. had two little people following him around. My mother, who is truly a saint, watched all three youngsters and also looked after the needs of her husband and other children, while maintaining a gigantic three-story house that had an oval-shaped ballroom and a billiard room in the basement. Eleven of us lived in that house, and my mother did all of the cooking, cleaning, and laundry. She had a saying, that by doing good works, she was piling up jewels for her heavenly crown. She certainly earned every one of them.

The year Charlie graduated from college, we moved our small family into a house of our own, and I couldn't have been happier. Charlie had landed a job he wanted, making exhibits at the St. Paul Science Museum at a starting salary of $400 a month. That wasn't much, even in 1961, but our house cost only $14,900. My father had a banker friend who arranged the mortgage. It wasn't the house of my dreams, and I always considered it a "starter" house, but it was ours—a snug stucco bungalow on Roblyn Avenue in St. Paul, with three bedrooms upstairs and an apple tree in the backyard. There was no thought of me working from then on, at least not outside the home. When I wanted a piano, I purchased one on time payments and began giving piano lessons. (Charlie was pretty surprised the day the piano arrived; I hadn't yet told him about it and how I planned to pay for it.) After the piano was paid for, I started putting money away for a down payment on the house I *really* wanted in the country.

The year after we moved into that snug bungalow, three months after our daughter Jane was born in the spring of 1963, Charlie was badly injured in a rock slide in Montana.

He was on a dinosaur dig for the Science Museum, helping excavate its famous triceratops. Charlie called me on the night of July 3 to say that he was in the hospital in Jordan, Montana, but told me not to worry. On hearing the news, my father told me I belonged out there with Charlie, no question. The next day, the Fourth of July, he took me to the train station in St. Paul and gave me fifty silver dollars—part of a stash he had been hoarding since the United States had gone off the silver standard and the only cash he had on hand over the holiday—to pay for my ticket to Miles City, Montana, the nearest railroad station to Jordan, eighty miles away.

The lone nurse from the hospital in Jordan picked me up in Miles City, drove me to Jordan, and helped me settle into Charlie's double room. That Jordan even had a hospital is amazing because the town's main street was still unpaved, but it did, a brand-new brick building. The one doctor on staff, Doc Ferrin, was the spitting image of old Doc Adams on the television program *Gunsmoke.* For putting me up and also providing all of my meals, the hospital charged our insurance company $2.50 per day. Charlie quickly became something of a celebrity in town and received lots of visitors bearing gifts of books and flowers, anxious to talk with a dinosaur digger.

Doc Ferrin kept Charlie in traction for three weeks in Jordan before I brought him back on the train to undergo reconstructive hip surgery at Midway Hospital in St. Paul. From there he came home to Roblyn Avenue in a body cast, in which he remained encased for the next several months. I equipped a second-floor bedroom for him with a rented hospital bed and small black-and-white TV. In that room, a few days before Thanksgiving on November 22, we watched the horrible unfolding news that President Kennedy had been shot in Dallas. Thirty years later, on November 22,

1993, our daughter Jane would be shot to death on this same terrible day. In 1963, with Charlie unable to move from his bed, I carried Thanksgiving dinner for our young family upstairs and we ate in his small room.

The seven years we lived on Roblyn Avenue in St. Paul went by quickly. In one of my favorite flashbacks, Patty and

Charles and Patty

Charles are chasing butterflies with butterfly nets in our backyard, followed by their father, his own butterfly net in hand, trying to keep up with them on crutches. The neighborhood was full of small children, and ours made close friends. Our house was near the Town and Country Club, where my father had a membership, and the children liked splashing in its wading pool. When it snowed, Charlie and I took them sliding on the steep hills of the club's golf course. This was how life was supposed to be, and it was a good era in which to be raising children. When Patty started kindergarten at St. Mark's School, seven blocks away, she walked to and from school. I didn't have a car. Can you imagine sending a child that young out to walk to school today?

Until Patty started school, we didn't have a clock in the house. We never got around to buying one. I actually have a strong dislike for clocks, and to this day avoid them as much as possible. I never have a clock in a room in which

I am writing. When it got light in the morning, Charlie would get up and drive downtown to work. When his coworkers went home, he usually did too. He was one of only seven employees at the museum in those early days.

Today the Science Museum (now the Science Museum of Minnesota) has several hundred people on staff and has recently completed a new seventy million-dollar facility. This is actually the third new museum building since Charlie started there. The first Science Museum in which he worked was housed in a red sandstone mansion built in 1887 for Colonel John Merriam (father of Minnesota governor William Merriam). That building stood a few hundred feet north of the Minnesota State Capitol. One of Charlie's treasures—he keeps it on the desk in his library—is a red stone gargoyle head that he salvaged from the exterior trim of the Merriam house when it was razed.

Charlie had graduated from art school with a degree in graphic design, but his real love has always been painting and sculpture. Nights and weekends on Roblyn Avenue, he was always busy in his basement studio with projects of his own. Working in clay, he modeled a series of small Eskimo sculptures that he cast in plaster and painted. He sold these and other small sculptures of hunters and fishermen to Crossroads of Sport in New York, a prestigious sporting art firm that issued handsome hardcover catalogs. Once, when it came time to send a shipment of pieces to New York, I asked him if we could drive them out by car. So we left Patty and Charles with my parents on Lake Harriet, and Charlie's mother watched Jane at her house in St. Paul. We had been thinking of building a house in the country and were considering an A-frame, but we came back from the East with plans for a Colonial-style house, similar to a whaling captain's house we had seen in Mystic Seaport, Connecticut.

All three of our children were in school—Jane was just starting kindergarten—and I was very pregnant with our youngest, Mary Susan, when we moved to our present home in rural Afton. The price of land has sky-rocketed in Afton in recent years, but our five wooded acres cost us only four thousand dollars, less than we would have paid for a city lot in St. Paul. Mary was born three weeks after we moved in, and with the older children in school, I had more time to enjoy this last baby. I also had plenty of time to decorate my dream house. I stained woodwork and papered and painted walls with abandon until I ran out of rooms.

Our children: Mary Susan, Patty, Jane, Charles

While Mary was still a toddler, I talked Charlie into helping me start a limited edition print and framing business from our home. Charlie made hand-silk-screened wildlife art prints that I framed and sold through our own mail-order catalog and to art galleries. I took Mary along with me when I called on Twin Cities galleries. I still didn't have a car, so this meant driving Charlie a half hour to work in the morning and picking him up at night so that I could use his. Once a year, we invited friends and customers to our home to see his new paintings and prints, and he also had one-man shows in several galleries.

One day while I was framing a large print, thinking into the future, I wondered what I would be doing when I was, say, seventy. Would I still be up in this studio over our attached garage, framing pictures? I liked the work, I enjoyed picking out matting and framing materials, putting colors and textures together. Framing wasn't hard work for me then, but would I still be able to lift heavy pieces of glass, for instance, when I was older? Would my eyesight be good enough to cut perfectly mitered inside mat corners? I was in my mid-thirties, and I still didn't have a clue that I would be a writer.

Our art business boomed, but Charlie lost interest in it after a few years. He didn't like commercial demands on his time. He especially hated going to his own art shows. He actually quit painting for a time. Mary had started school, and I was casting about for ways to occupy my new-found time. A wife's role was to care for her husband and children, we had been taught at St. Joe's. I had always assumed that anything I did beyond raising children would be to help further Charlie's career. Now he didn't want any help. He had left the Science Museum and taken a job with the Department of the Interior, developing and designing exhibit programs for wildlife refuges throughout the fifty states. His job entailed a good deal of travel, including trips to Alaska and Hawaii, which I envied just a little. One of his colleagues took his wife on the trip to Alaska, but there was no question of my going with four small children at home.

In my quandary about something to do beyond house-work, one day I hit upon the bright idea of trying to write a magazine article.

2

Cereal Ads and Cider

THE THOUGHT OF ACTUALLY selling an article seemed like pie in the sky to me, but what did I have to lose? I had seen a copy of a new magazine called *Americana* at a friend's art gallery, and I thought I had a good idea for an article. For the past couple of years, I had been collecting early Cream of Wheat ads. It would be fun to see if I could write an article about them for *Americana*.

Cream of Wheat advertisements were in a class by themselves. During the early 1900s, the Cream of Wheat Company had waged one of the most successful campaigns in the history of American advertising, commissioning paintings by some of this country's finest illustrators. James Montgomery Flagg painted for Cream of Wheat. So did J. C. Leyendecker, Philip R. Goodwin, Jessie Willcox Smith, and N. C. Wyeth. The full-page advertisements appeared monthly in national magazines including *Collier's, The Saturday Evening Post*, and *The Delineator*. Three Cream of Wheat paintings, two by Wyeth and one by Goodwin, now hang in the Minneapolis Institute of Arts.

I had discovered my first Cream of Wheat ad loose on a table in the basement of Harold's Book Shop on West Seventh Street in St. Paul. Clipped from a vintage magazine, the ad featured a painting by artist G. J. Perrett of Uncle Sam extolling Cream of Wheat during World War I. Titled *Well, You're Helping Some*, it reminded me of James Montgomery Flagg's famous poster painting, *Uncle Sam Needs You*. I bought the ad for a dollar or two, with the idea that I could frame it for our kitchen.

Not long afterward, at an antiques store, I found two more Cream of Wheat ads, both of them by St. Paul artist Edward V. Brewer. One of them pictured a stork delivering a baby to the Cream of Wheat Inn; a note tacked to the front door read: "Boy Wanted." In the second ad, titled *Financially Embarrassed*, a little boy stands before a grocery store counter, searching his pockets in vain for money to buy a box of Cream of Wheat.

The Brewer ads brought back a rush of memories. Charlie and I had known Ed Brewer when we lived in St. Paul. He had lived about a mile from us on the other side of the Town and Country Club golf course. I had met him when he played host to a group of piano teachers that included me at his home and studio one fine summer day. I remembered where I had seen Cream of Wheat ads before. It was at Ed Brewer's house, and lo and behold, I recognized the Cream of Wheat Inn pictured in his "Boy Wanted" advertisement. It was Ed's own stucco-and-timbers studio.

Ed Brewer had come to fame as a much sought-after

portrait painter for Minnesota's rich and famous. Before that, however, as a starting-out artist, he had painted several dozen Cream of Wheat ads between about 1911 and 1926. He actually painted more Cream of Wheat ads than any other artist. His winsome ads often featured one or more of his three children.

The Cream of Wheat company kept all of the original paintings, but Ed showed our piano teachers group one that he had retrieved. It was a picture of a tiny, tired newsboy,

sitting with his dog and an armful of Cream of Wheat circulars at the base of a statue of Lincoln. The newsboy was his small son David, Ed said, and the painting, *Mighty Oaks from Tiny Acorns Grow,* had been his wife Ida's favorite.

When Ida was dying with cancer in 1961, Ed had tried to buy back or borrow the painting. Company officials took their time deliberating. The painting finally arrived one day at Ed's door, but it was too late. Ida hadn't lived to see it come home. Ed hung onto it, and Cream of Wheat never asked for it back.

Some weeks after first meeting Ed, I called him in a panic. I had been in our basement on Roblyn Avenue doing laundry while the children played outside with the hose. All of a sudden, I noticed water coming into the basement through an open window, and I grabbed an oil painting that was getting wet. We stored anything and everything in our basement, and this canvas, which belonged to a friend, was down there, waiting for Charlie to clean it. My hasty attempt to rescue it from water, however, resulted in my catching it on some protuberance—I don't remember what—and poking a hole through it.

Minutes later, Ed Brewer was at our door to pick up the damaged painting. Not to worry, he said. He could mend it as good as new. When he returned with it several days later, he had not only repaired the tear but had also cleaned the painting (saving Charlie the trouble). His fee, he said, was fifteen dollars.

Ed Brewer was a grand old man, slender and graceful, and still handsome, charming, and popular with the ladies in his eighties. We invited him to dinner several times at our house, and on those occasions, our three children could barely contain themselves. After dinner, they knew, he would show them "how money slips through your fingers," his favorite trick. One at a time, the youngsters would be asked to hold out a thumb and forefinger, about an inch apart. Then Ed would hold a dollar in midair between the outreached fingers. If the child caught the bill when Ed let it go, it was his or hers to keep. Their tiny fingers usually did not react quickly enough, but each child always ended up with a dollar bill anyway.

In those days, Ed drove a long, sleek gold-colored Cadillac. He had extended his garage to accommodate it. Somehow the big automobile seemed to make up for the time during the Depression when a hospital had taken his much more modest car for a bill he was slow in paying.

St. Paul newspaperman Gareth Hiebert wrote about Ed in his "Oliver Towne" column, and Charlie and I saw him the same evening the article appeared. We expected him to be in high spirits because the piece had been highly complimentary, but he wasn't pleased. Instead Ed was peeved that Hiebert had mentioned that he was eighty-four. "People will think I'm too old to paint," he fretted, and he was still soliciting commissions.

Several years later, after we had moved to Afton, finding the two Brewer Cream of Wheat ads set me on a quest. I hunted for Cream of Wheat ads everywhere I might hope to find them, mostly at antiques stores and flea markets. Once, on a trip west, Charlie and I stopped at a home in North Dakota, where I purchased dozens of early magazines with Cream of Wheat ads from a man who had found them behind his walls when insulating his house. I usually paid anywhere from fifty cents to a couple of dollars apiece for the ads, and I was continually amazed at their diversity.

A very early and very charming 1902 series was based on nursery rhymes: Little Miss Muffet, Little Boy Blue, Mistress Mary Quite Contrary, and Old King Cole all touted the cereal. Each year at Christmastime, Santa Claus sang the praises of Cream of Wheat, and many of the ads featured the black chef Rastus. In 1906 Rastus was depicted as a sort of Pied Piper— clad in tartan, carrying bagpipes (along with his box of cereal), and leading a merry band of children. Several ads picture Rastus's beaming face on a billboard advertisement for Cream of Wheat that is part of the composition. I framed twenty-five or thirty of my favorite ads for the half bath off our kitchen.

When I told Charlie that I would like to try to write a magazine article, he went out and bought me a typewriter, a heavy old black manual machine he found for $39.99 at the AAA Typewriter Company, now long defunct, in downtown St. Paul. (The Cream of Wheat article was the only one I ever typed on it.) Charlie also helped me with information about some of the Cream of Wheat artists. He has been collecting books since he was twelve and has a fine library. One of his special interests is American art history.

One book Charlie handed me was *The Wyeths* by Betsy Wyeth, N. C. Wyeth's daughter-in-law, which contains excerpts from the young artist's letters to

Rip Van Winkle *by Ed Brewer*

his mother. N. C. was fresh out of Howard Pyle's Brandywine Art School in 1906 when he wrote home:

> Mr. Mapes of the Cream of Wheat Co. telegraphed for me to run up and see him at the Waldorf-Astoria. He is the owner of that famous cereal co., and is a man of immense wealth. I have just completed two pictures for him, $250 each, which he is immensely pleased with.

These paintings were *The Bronco Buster* and *Rural Delivery*, and both now hang in the Minneapolis Institute of Arts. N. C. also painted a third Cream of Wheat painting,

The Bronco Buster *by N. C. Wyeth*

The Yukon Freighter, in 1907. The painting was five feet high and three feet wide. N. C. called it "a whopper of a picture," which it definitely was, and not only because of its size. This first-rate canvas pictured a parka-clad Eskimo, riding a dogsled lashed with freight, including a wooden crate of Cream of Wheat, fighting off a pack of hungry wolves with his gunstock. All three Wyeth paintings were later donated to the Minneapolis Institute of Arts, but *The Yukon Freighter* was destroyed by fire when it was sent out to be restored in 1969.

For background on the cereal company, I wrote to Nabisco, Inc., in New Jersey, which purchased Cream of Wheat about 1960. I received back a pamphlet that explained how Cream of Wheat had originated in a small flour mill in Grand Forks, North Dakota. The mill had been facing ruin in 1893, when the wife of one of the millers concocted a breakfast porridge from the middlings of the wheat berry. The millers sent ten cases of "Cream of Wheat" to New York with their next shipment of flour. The response was immediate: "Forget the flour," wrote the brokers, "and send us a carload of Cream of Wheat." By 1897 demand for the cereal had outstripped the capacity of the small mill, and the company moved to Minneapolis.

Once I had assembled my research material (which for this article consisted primarily of the ads themselves and biographical material concerning the artists), it took me only three days to write the Cream of Wheat piece. This amazed even me. Was magazine writing really this easy? One answer is that by this time, I knew quite a lot about my subject, and my enthusiasm for it was fierce. I was sure that I had hit on a fascinating subject that would interest others as it did me (which is what a magazine article has to do, of course). I mailed my carefully typed manuscript of seven double-spaced pages, along with a self-addressed stamped envelope, to editor Michael Durham at *Americana* magazine in New York in late December 1975.

In January, a letter from Michael Durham on *Americana* letterhead stationery sent me into a state of euphoria. This was the first letter I had ever received from a magazine editor, and he hadn't returned my manuscript!

> I enjoyed your manuscript on the Cream of Wheat ads [Durham wrote], but before coming to a definite decision about it, I would like to see the photographs you mentioned in your letter. Could you send them to us as soon as possible?

Again I turned to Charlie, who had studied photography in art school. Charlie took a roll of color slides of some of my best ads, and I mailed them to Durham posthaste. Was it possible, I allowed myself to contemplate, that this first article of mine would actually sell?!

Durham acknowledged receipt of the pictures in February and said that he hoped to be able to go over them and the manuscript more carefully soon. During the days and weeks that followed, my life took on new meaning as I looked forward to the mail each day with mounting excitement. The long-awaited envelope from *Americana* finally arrived in mid-April, and it was good news.

Durham would be happy to accept the article, he said, "once we have figured out a way to overcome the somewhat delicate problem of Rastus. We have to assume that the Rastus figure is going to offend some reader. . . . When and why did the company drop him as an advertising symbol? . . . Once you have taken care of the Rastus problem . . . we will pay you $250."

Happy day! My article was as good as sold! Rastus was really no problem at all. One of the best-known faces in America, the benevolent chef remains to this day Cream of Wheat's symbol of hospitality. No racial slur was intended, and none that I know of has ever been taken, I explained. To make this point clear, I revised my article to include even more material about Rastus.

In 1914 Ed Brewer had produced a painting titled *A Proud Day for Rastus*. This was actually a self-portrait of Brewer sculpting the bust of a black Pullman car chef-waiter he had hired to pose for him. Until that time, Rastus had only been depicted full face, but from this time on, the three-dimensional model allowed Brewer to paint the chef in a variety of poses. A 1922 Brewer ad titled *An Old Friend* depicts a portrait of Rastus in a gold frame, hanging in an art museum.

"Thank you for the new version of the Cream of Wheat ads article," Michael Durham wrote to me on April 29. "There might be another idea in your caveat about preserving paper Americana at the end of the manuscript. A short service article perhaps." So began a long and happy relationship with Michael Durham and *Americana* during which I wrote a variety of articles for this magazine. More often than not, the ideas for the articles were mine, but Durham also continued to suggest service articles such as "How to Care for Oil Paintings," "How to Take Care of Silver and Pewter," and so on.

I used my first $250 check from *Americana* to help make the first payment on my first car—a metallic gold-colored Volkswagen Dasher that I drove until it rusted out about ten years later. That car was my pride and joy, and it was also a good investment in my budding career. There is no public transportation in Afton or from Afton to the Twin Cities, so if you don't have a car, you just don't go very far. With the Dasher, I was suddenly able to do research at Twin Cities libraries. I began showing up regularly at the St. Paul Public Library, the James Jerome Hill Reference Library next door, and the Minnesota Historical Society. Sometimes when I was between ideas for articles, I'd go to a library and browse the stacks until I got one.

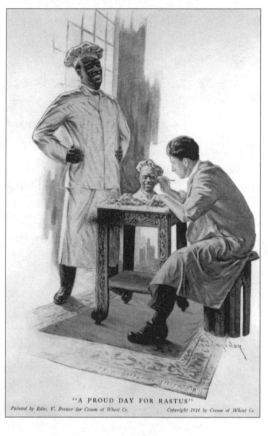

"A PROUD DAY FOR RASTUS"

Painted by Edw. V. Brewer for Cream of Wheat Co.   *Copyright 1914 by Cream of Wheat Co.*

After selling that first magazine article, there was no stopping me. This was the most fun I had ever had. What else could I write about? I pondered one day while I was baking an apple pie. I have always liked making pies. I especially like rolling out the flaky crusts and fluting the tender piecrust edges. There's something very satisfying, even therapeutic, about making a handsome pie. If I couldn't make a living any other way, I would like to make and sell "Pat's Pies."

While I was still shaping that particular pie, I realized

that there was probably a good story in the history of apples. I had to wait until the pie came out of the oven, but then I hurried down to our local library to start finding out about this favorite fruit.

I learned some amazing facts. Was an apple the forbidden fruit in the Garden of Paradise? The Bible doesn't say so. It's more likely, some scholars propose, that Eve bit into an apricot or an orange, maybe a fig. Stone Age people in Europe did eat apples, however, and also preserved them by sun-drying them. Eons later, apples were one of the first fruits to be domesticated and were cultivated by the Greeks and Romans. The Greeks believed that their gods retained their eternal youth by eating golden apples. The Romans carried apples to all the countries their legions conquered. In Britain, apples soon became the major fruit crop.

The first apple seeds arrived in America aboard the *Mayflower,* and the first apple orchard in the New World was planted on Beacon Hill by a Boston clergyman. The Dutch brought apples to New York, the French scattered seeds and plants along the St. Lawrence River, and Spanish priests established orchards at their missions in what is now the southwestern United States. Creek, Cherokee, and Choctaw Indians all planted apple orchards at their villages. By the time the colonies became the United States of America, apples were this nation's fruit of choice.

The overwhelming popularity of the apple in colonial America was due in large part to cider—a tart, mildly alcoholic beverage comparable to today's hard cider—which colonists ingested in large quantities. In an era before the complexities of bacteriology had been unraveled, our forefathers believed that many human ills were traced to drinking water. This was not surprising. In Europe the waters had been polluted by every manner of filth. In Elizabethan

England, it was common practice to dump even the contaminated bedclothes of plague victims into the nearest body of water. So despite an abundance of fresh, untainted water on this side of the Atlantic, colonists turned to home-brewed beers and wines, and apple cider became the favorite drink in colonial America.

Colonial housewives baked, fried, and stewed apples to accompany almost every meal, serving apple pie even for breakfast, and they used cider vinegar for pickling—one of the most common methods of preserving food. One New Jersey Scot named Laird learned how to distill cider to make apple brandy, better known as applejack, and launched a family business. Physicians prescribed apple spirits for sedatives, stimulants, antiseptics, and even as an anesthetic during surgery.

Thanks to helpful librarians, I soon had enough information from which to construct a brief article of about two thousand words. I also knew where I could probably sell my apples story, having recently purchased a copy of *Writer's Market*. This book is updated annually and contains listings for magazines and book publishers throughout the country: name, address, contact person, information about the types of material published, payment, and so on. *Writer's Market* opened many doors in my new world of writing, and I kept it on my nightstand for years.

One of the magazines listed in *Writer's Market* was *Early American Life*, which sounded like a good candidate for my story because of the strong association between apples and colonial America. So with that magazine in mind, I began by writing down what I considered to be the most interesting facts about apples, focusing on their role in colonial America.

Once I had all my interesting facts on paper, I cut them apart, spread them out on the floor, and began piecing them together, mostly chronologically, to form a coherent narrative. (This kind of thing is much easier to do today with a word processor, but back then it was largely a matter of cut and tape.) I ended my article with apple recipes that I obtained from the American Apple Institute in Washington, D.C.

Before typing my final draft, I bought a new type-writer. Typing on my manual machine was never easy, and it produced uneven copy because I was unable to strike all the keys with equal force. So I went back to the neighbor-hood where I had grown up in St. Paul and the drugstore on Selby Avenue where I had met Charlie. The drugstore was now an office supplies store, and for three hundred dollars, I purchased an electric typewriter, on which I would write hundreds of magazine articles.

Early American Life purchased the apples article ("Apples and Cider") for $250, and asked me if I would write an arti-cle about Benjamin Franklin and fire insurance. Of course I would. I had no idea what Benjamin Franklin had to do with fire insurance, but I didn't suppose it would take me long to find out. A public librarian pointed me to The Philadelphia Contributionship for the Insurance of Houses from Loss by Fire, the first successful fire insurance company in the American colonies. Franklin had helped found it in 1752, and it was still in existence.

I fired off a letter to Philadelphia Contributionship secretary and treasurer Walter L. Smith, Jr., who responded by outlining for me the importance of fire insurance:

> Fire insurance [he explained] brought not only peace of mind to our colonial society, but also encouraged the acquisi-tion of property and the investment in property by lenders on mortgages. As a result the economy was able to expand rapidly and today fire insurance is regarded as the corner-stone on which the entire property insurance industry has been built.

Benjamin Franklin was concerned his whole life with the subject of fire, I learned. As a child of five, in 1711, he had experienced the horror of the Boston Towne House Fire, which destroyed more than a hundred houses along with shops, churches, and stores. Years later he reminded readers in his *Gazette:* "You may be forced (as I once was) to leap out of your windows and hazard your neck to avoid being over-roasted."

Following that catastrophic Boston fire, many local homeowners banded together to form mutual aid societies to assist the town's paid engine companies. Each volunteer member equipped himself with a bag (to salvage valuables), a bucket, and a bed key. Beds were usually the most valuable pieces of furniture a family owned, and with the wrench-like bed key, they could be unbolted and carried outside in sections.

Franklin patterned Philadelphia's first volunteer fire department—the Union Fire Company—after these early Boston societies, and the Union Fire Company led to The Philadelphia Contributionship. One half of the new fire insurance company's board of directors had been among Franklin's volunteer firemen. The Contributionship insured houses within ten miles of Philadelphia, but it would not insure houses that had trees within sixty feet of them. Ben was convinced by his experiments with electricity that green trees attracted lightning. Trees, moreover, prevented the wooden hand pumpers of the day from getting close to a house afire.

The Contributionship remained the only fire insurance company in colonial America for thirty years until a second American company, The Mutual Assistance Company, opened its books in Philadelphia in 1784. For a slightly higher rate, this firm would also insure homes with shade trees.

It probably had to, since the Contributionship had previously insured nearly every other house in town. During the next fifteen years, one city after another—New York, Baltimore, Charleston, Providence, Hartford, and other East Coast communities—founded local fire insurance companies.

The bibliography in my file for this article lists six books and assorted pamphlets, so I did a lot of reading. What I was doing must be a lot like writing papers for college classes, I mused. One difference was that I was being paid while I was learning. Instead of receiving grades, I was receiving checks. As soon as I completed the fire insurance piece, I began another for *Early American Life,* a piece I suggested titled "All About Lilacs." Lilacs, I had discovered, were the favorite dooryard shrub in colonial America, so this subject too was a natural for this magazine.

I had never taken any writing classes with the exception of journalism in high school. I used to think long and hard about going back to school, but I'm uncomfortable in any type of classroom setting, don't ask me why. I don't like sitting in any kind of a group for very long. I wouldn't like the wasted time of going to and from classes, which would be considerable, given that I live a half hour from the Twin Cities in Afton.

Instead, over the years, I have read dozens of books about writing in search of inspiration and practical advice. The practical advice came from books such as *The Elements of Style* by William Strunk, Jr. and E. B. White and *On Writing Well* by William Zinsser. Books about writers provided the inspiration, books like *One Writer's Beginnings* by Eudora Welty. Miss Welty was a shy and reticent short-story writer and novelist. Her work explored the human relationships and regional manners of the inhabitants of a small Southern town, not unlike her own birthplace of Jackson, Mississippi. She won a Pulitzer Prize for *The Optimist's Daughter*, published in 1972.

Magazines for writers were another good avenue of information for me. After selling the Cream of Wheat piece, I subscribed to *The Writer*. I remember looking forward to each month's new magazine and sitting down immediately with it when it arrived in the mail. In addition to articles, this magazine also listed a few markets. One of the first issues I received contained a notice that *Persimmon Hill* magazine was seeking articles about American western artists. Talk about coincidence! Charlie and I had been collecting artwork by Philip R. Goodwin and had gone to great lengths to learn more about him.

Our Goodwin collection began with an oil painting Charlie acquired from an art gallery in St. Paul and includes watercolors and small sculptures we have purchased from various sources, usually galleries out west. Philip Goodwin was a close friend of Charlie Russell's and painted with him on several trips to Montana. One of our treasures was an illustrated letter Goodwin wrote to Russell following one of these trips. We found this at Trailside Galleries in Jackson Hole. (My Cream of Wheat collection also includes the single Cream of Wheat ad Goodwin painted.)

Not much had been written about Goodwin. At seventeen, young Phil had been a promising student at Howard Pyle's Brandywine Art School (where his classmates included Frank Schoonover and N. C. Wyeth), and he afterward had a studio in New York. He painted advertisements and covers for *The Saturday Evening Post*, *Collier's Weekly*, *McClure's*, and *Everybody's* magazines and illustrated many books, among them *The Call of the Wild* by Jack London and *African Game Trails* by Theodore Roosevelt.

Goodwin's paintings were always outdoor action scenes that included wildlife, and his dramatic calendar prints were familiar to two generations of sportsmen. Numerous museums (including the Amon Carter in Fort Worth, the Thomas Gilcrease Institute in Tulsa, and the Whitney Gallery of Western Art in Cody, Wyoming) had acquired Goodwin oil and watercolor paintings. His artwork was well known, but the man was not.

A "Bear" Chance *by Philip R. Goodwin*

In our personal search for Philip Goodwin, however, Charlie and I had located the one person on the planet who knew more about him than anyone else. We had tracked down Neva Goodwin, his brother's widow, who lived in California, and driven there to visit her. Mrs. Goodwin showed us scrapbooks filled with sketches, photographs, and newspaper articles that chronicled Goodwin's career in New York and his frequent trips into the wilderness, habitat he clearly preferred. Tied neatly in bundles were letters he had written home to his mother. The story of Philip R. Goodwin's life was contained in a trunk that had come to Neva and her husband following Phil's death from pneumonia in 1935 at the relatively young age of fifty-four.

This was a story no one else had, and I realized that

it was probably perfect for *Persimmon Hill*, which was published by the National Cowboy Hall of Fame in Oklahoma
City. Like the Cream of Wheat article, it almost wrote itself,
it was that easy. I mailed my manuscript to editor Dean
Krakel at *Persimmon Hill* on January 14, 1977. Krakel
responded immediately (his letter is dated January 18) and
thanked me for submitting it.

> I enjoyed it a great deal [he wrote]. In fact, I found it
> refreshing after reading so many rather dull manuscripts. . . .
> We are pretty well stacked up with art articles [but] I am going
> to see how it might fit in. . . . Lord only knows, Goodwin
> deserves some attention in print.

Krakel was as good as his word: "In Search of Philip R.
Goodwin" appeared in the Spring 1978 issue of *Persimmon Hill.*

*Philip R. Goodwin in his studio in
Mamaroneck, New York*

After reading it, a man named John Brendel, who lived at the Sea Horse Mobile Home Park in St. Petersburg, sent me a collection of about eighty Goodwin prints of varying sizes, some of them quite large, that he had purchased at a New York frame shop in the 1940s. He wanted someone who would appreciate them to have them, he said. I'm still taking very good care of them.

By the late 1970s I was also selling quite a few articles to *American History Illustrated* magazine. These included pieces titled "A Lovely Life: The life and work of Jessie Wilcox Smith" (another artist who painted for Cream of Wheat); "Seth Eastman: Pictorial Historian" (which led almost twenty years later to a book on this subject by the Afton Historical Society Press); "St. Paul's Celebration of Snow, the Winter Carnival" (the subject of another Afton Historical Society Press book); and "A Cowboy's Christmas" (about the Christmas cards Charlie Russell painted and sent to his friends).

Much of what I was learning about writing for magazines was coming from the editors I was working with. Every time one of my articles was published, I compared it—word for word, comma for comma—with my original manuscript to see what had been changed or corrected. I thought of editors as something akin to gods, but I learned that they too could occasionally make a mistake.

One of my articles for *Americana* magazine was titled "How to Cook a Buffalo." Charlie had recently completed a series of large paintings of prairie animals for Fort Niobrara Wildlife Refuge outside Valentine, Nebraska, where we had observed the refuge's annual spring buffalo auction. My manuscript promoted buffalo as being healthier than beef, and I explained that buffalo meat had been a staple on the American frontier.

Pemmican [I wrote] had been the most popular Indian method of preparing and preserving buffalo. Sun-dried flakes of meat were pounded fine and mixed with melted fat, marrow, and sometimes, wild berries. Most often, the mixture was packed into a parfleche bag fashioned from a buffalo hide [and] the contents would keep for several years. . . . Boiled, it made a soup known to frontiersmen as "rubbaboo."

By the time my article appeared in the May/June issue of *Americana,* an editor had revised this material to read: "Pioneers used to boil dried buffalo chips into soup and call it rubbaboo, but cooking techniques have improved considerably since then." I should hope so! I fired off a quick letter to the editor that appeared in the September/October issue:

Your edited version of my article provided me with quite a chuckle. I refer to the sentence "Pioneers used to boil dried buffalo chips into soup and call it rubbaboo." Buffalo chips are akin to cow pies—great round mounds of manure. They burned well and were used as firewood on the treeless prairie.

But editors also suggested ways to make my articles better, pushing me to delve deeper into my subject matter. Michael Durham at *Americana* was one of these people; Pamela Herr at *The American West* magazine was another. In May 1977 I proposed an article about Roland Reed, who had photographed American Indians at the turn of the century, to *The American West.* A collection of Reed's glass plate negatives and handwritten notes concerning the images had recently been purchased by Kramer Gallery in St. Paul.

Thank you for your recent letter suggesting an article on Roland Reed [Ms. Herr replied]. The subject does appear to be both interesting and appropriate for *The American West.* However, since we are a small publication without extensive financial resources, the article would have to be done on speculation.

That sounded fine to me. I wanted to be published in *The American West*. It was a scholarly and beautiful magazine sponsored by the prestigious Western History Association. I would be glad to write the article on speculation, I informed Ms. Herr. The Reed photographs were extraordinary, and given the firsthand information available to me, I was confident that I could produce a first-rate article. She could expect to see it within a month, I wrote.

After completing and sending off my manuscript as promised, I heard from Pamela Herr in early August:

We liked your manuscript on Roland Reed very much but want to suggest a few revisions before accepting it.

1) Edward Curtis photographed the American Indian at about the same time as Reed; it would be helpful to mention Curtis in your article and briefly compare his aims and work to Reed's. (Please see the attached article on Curtis by Josephy.)

2) Reed's pictures seem to reflect to some extent a late-nineteenth-century idealization—even sentimentalization—of the Indian. It would be very appropriate to discuss this new and more sympathetic view of the Indian, first in general terms and then as it affected Reed's work. (See *The Reformers and the American Indian* by

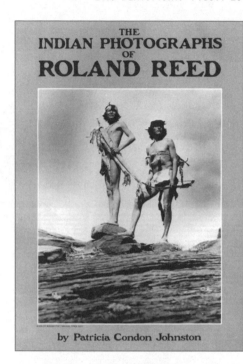

The title page from my first article for *The American West*, with Roland Reed photo, *Sons of Manuelita (Navajo 1913)*

Tribute to the Dead *(Piegan 1912)*

Robert Winston Mardock, University of Missouri Press, 1971.) There appears to be some conflict between Reed's careful arrangement of his Indian subjects for a handsome "story" effect (as in "The Wooing") and his desire for authenticity. (Josephy makes a very interesting point relating to this on page 57 of the Curtis article.) Are there any comments on this problem in Reed's notebooks? Page 7 might be a good place to discuss both points 1 and 2, which together help place Reed in a historical context.

3) You also might make a little more of Reed's sacrifice of his prosperous studio (again, like Curtis) in order to photograph Indians. In your original letter to us you made a nice dramatic point of this, and it would be effective in the article.

Once these revisions are completed (and their thrust is to provide a broader background for your discussion of Reed's work), we will be pleased to accept the article for publication. Payment will be $200.

The Wooing *(Ojibwe, 1908)*

With this kind of generous help, it would be hard for a writer to fail. Pamela Herr had laid out exactly what I needed to do to complete a winning article. "The Indian Photographs of Roland Reed" appeared in the March/April 1978 issue of *The American West*, illustrated with a stunning fourteen-page portfolio of Reed photographs. I am proud of it to this day.

Many of my articles relied heavily on the illustrations that accompanied them. Often I provided them. Charlie

White Wolf *(Cheyenne, 1913)*

photographed some of our Goodwin artwork for the
Persimmon Hill article. He also took color slides of the Seth
Eastman watercolor paintings at the James J. Hill Reference
Library in St. Paul for the *American History Illustrated* article.
Other times, I made arrangements to borrow images from
museums, libraries, art galleries, or private collectors.
Kramer Gallery provided the photographs for the Roland
Reed article, for instance.

I loved my new life as a writer, and I was developing
a passion for American art and history. One story idea
seemed to spawn another. Writing was taking up all of my
daytime hours while Charlie was at work and the younger
children were in school. Patty and Charles had graduated
from high school by this time and gone off to college, Patty
to Utah State in Logan, Charles to Notre Dame in South
Bend, Indiana. Once they were both in college, I began to
wonder if I shouldn't be thinking about college for myself.
On more than one occasion, a lack of scholarly credentials
threatened to hamper my fledgling career.

3

A Mummy Dressed in Moccasins

I HAD ALREADY WRITTEN several articles for *Early American Life* when I queried the editors about a piece concerning itinerant portrait painter William Matthew Prior. Prior was one of hundreds of nineteenth-century folk artists who traveled from town to New England town painting portraits, but he was also unique in his time. Prior painted very competently in the polished, "academic" style of portrait painters such as Thomas Sully and Gilbert Stuart, but he more often worked in the "flat" primitive style associated with folk art. According to his newspaper advertisements, Prior's style of painting depended upon his fee. His paintings in both styles are contained in several museum collections.

"We've considered doing an article on itinerant portrait painters," assistant editor Patricia Faust replied to my proposal, "but feel that the author should be a professional in the art field. This holds true for any subject that has a high level of collector appeal."

This didn't put me off. "I really want to write this piece," I responded immediately, and I listed several articles I had written on American art subjects including the Cream of Wheat, Roland Reed, and others. "I can give you the best piece you've seen yet from me," I promised. "How about it?"

Ms. Faust replied by asking to see an outline of my article and suggestions for illustrations, which I sent, but she remained unconvinced.

"My feelings are still strong to have a museum curator take on an art piece," she wrote. "I'd be willing to see a manuscript on Prior on speculation, with you knowing in advance that I'll pass it along to our material culture consultant and that I'll rely on his opinion." This was fine with me, and I went ahead and wrote the article, which *Early American Life* purchased.

"William Matthew Prior: Itinerant Portrait Painter" ended up being the cover story for the June 1979 issue of *Early American Life*. Ms. Faust sent me a nice note:

The William Prior has turned out to be one of my favorites. I've ordered a dozen copies to be shipped to you with our compliments. Such successes as this article make everything hectic worthwhile.

I had much the same experience when I wanted to write an article about Swedish archeologist Gustaf Nordenskiold for *The American West*. Charlie and I had been prowling about out west when we became acquainted with Nordenskiold's extraordinary story at Mesa Verde National Park in Colorado. Not yet twenty-three years old and convalescing from tuberculosis when he traveled halfway around the world to explore the ancient Anasazi cliff dwellings in southwestern Colorado, Gustaf Nordenskiold would write the first major record of archeological work in the United States.

The sickly but intrepid son of Swedish scientist and explorer Adolf Erik Nordenskiold (who in 1878-79 was the first person to sail the long-searched-for Northwest Passage from Europe to the Orient), Gustaf had arrived unheralded at the Mancos Valley ranch of the Benjamin Wetherill family in a rented horse-drawn buggy in July 1891.

Gustaf Nordenskiold

In the preceding three years, Richard Wetherill, the oldest of Benjamin's five sons, had located, examined, and named all the major Mesa Verde cliff dwellings—by his own count, 182. The largest and most exqui-site was Cliff Palace. Spruce Tree House was named for a giant tree growing up through an outer retaining wall. He had also mapped the area, covering some two hundred fifty miles of the mesa's steep cliffs.

The Wetherills had already taken two significant collections of artifacts out of the ruins. The first—which went almost

Photo of cliff dwelling and man, probably Richard Wetherill, by Gustaf Nordenskiold

unnoticed until the mummy of a child was added to the assemblage of centuries-old pottery, clothing, tools, and weapons—had been pur-chased by the newly estab-lished Denver Historical Society, probably to keep it from being removed from the state. The second was still in storage in a small barn at the Wetherill ranch. Nobody was much interest-ed in the materials, and the

Wetherills' efforts had gone largely ignored in those quarters where they had hoped to gain support.

Nordenskiold was immediately drawn into their adventure and enthusiastically explored cliff house after cliff house, camping out with Richard and his brothers some distance from the ranch. "A large piece of sailcloth stretched between two trees is our bedroom, i.e. mine and my fore-man's," he wrote in one letter home to Sweden. "Two paces outside my room is a table, a real table, somewhat a la Robinson Crusoe, but nevertheless a table. A cloth—a piece of sailcloth, dirty and blotched—is spread over it."

At the end of the summer Nordenskiold returned to Sweden with nine boxes of "relics"—remains and artifacts numbering more than seven hundred individual items including a mummy dressed in moccasins and a skull cap. In 1892 he accompanied part of the collection to Spain for

Cliff dwellers' pottery found at Mesa Verde

the Columbus Jubilee. "I got a gold medal for the collection and the photos," he wrote to Richard Wetherill. He was also busy with his book. Illustrated with a superb portfolio of Nordenskiold's photographs, *The Cliff Dwellers of the Mesa Verde* was published in Stockholm and Chicago in 1893.

Unfortunately, Nordenskiold's health was deteriorating. "I have not been out of my bed since May 5th except the last days," he wrote to Richard Wetherill in June 1894. That fall he caught cold during a prolonged balloon flight and suffered a relapse of tuberculosis. When he grew worse during the winter, his doctors prescribed an extended stay at a sanatorium north of Stockholm. Accompanied by his wife and parents, Gustaf Nordenskiold was en route there by train when he died at Morsil Station in June 1895. Following the Columbus Jubilee exhibition in Spain, most of Gustaf Nordenskiold's Mesa Verde collection was acquired by a wealthy Finnish physician, and it is today housed in Finland's national museum. In 1958 the U.S. National Park Service, assisted by the National Geographic Society, began an intensive excavation project to learn more about Anasazi life in the prehistoric Colorado cliff dwellings. The Nordenskiold story was a very important one that I wanted to research and write, I wrote to Pamela Herr at *The American West*.

"We have considered your query very carefully and asked a member of our editorial board to give us his opinion as well," she replied in May 1978. But while she liked the subject matter, "I think such an article might most easily be done by an archeologist/anthropologist who could investigate the subject exhaustively and then offer an authoritative opinion on Nordenskiold's contribution. . . . If you do decide to go ahead with this on speculation, we would ask our editorial board expert for an evaluation, our usual procedure."

I spent happy days that summer assembling the Nordenskiold article with help from museum personnel in this country and Finland. After receiving my manuscript, Pamela Herr replied with several questions and comments.

Had I seen the correspondence between the Wetherills and the Smithsonian about sponsorship? she wanted to know. Yes, I had. That organization had replied to the Wetherills' request for help that it could do nothing at the time, but if the Wetherills cared to put together a collection, it would be glad to accept it.

Referring to my manuscript, Miss Herr's letter continued:

> Page 17: evidently the National Park Service does not have a collection of Mesa Verde artifacts—would you check this out, and also find out where the Mesa Verde artifacts in the U.S. are housed.

In fact, the National Park Service *did* have an extensive collection of Mesa Verde artifacts at that site. There are also other collections of Mesa Verde material at the Colorado Historical Society and the University of Pennsylvania. I incorporated these facts in my revised manuscript, and once again, with Ms. Herr's help, my final draft passed muster.

"Gustaf Nordenskiold and the Treasure of the Mesa Verde" was the cover story for the July/August 1979 issue of *The American West*. It was a gorgeous piece, illustrated with Nordenskiold's photographs and present-day color photographs taken at Mesa Vera by celebrated photographer David Muench.

In the case of both articles, the Prior and the Nordenski-old, I never questioned my ability to write them. I actually felt that I could probably produce a better article for these magazines than an "expert," simply because I wasn't one. I wasn't carrying any academic baggage or biases. I didn't know the technical jargon. Mine was a fresh viewpoint. What I turned up that interested me would probably also interest my readers, most of whom, like myself, were not academics.

I always worked very hard at producing the best articles possible, never stinting, first of all, on research. For one of my first articles for *Americana* magazine, Charlie drove me almost nine hundred miles to Denver to interview art collectors Bill and Dorothy Harmsen. The Harmsens had started the wildly successful Jolly Rancher Candy Company out of their ice cream shop in Golden, Colorado. After selling Jolly Rancher to Beatrice Foods, they had spent their profits assembling the largest collection of Western art west of the Mississippi.

We spent several days in Denver getting to know Bill and Dorothy. They took us to dinner at good restaurants and visited with us at their downtown Polo Club penthouse (where, outdoors, on their sky-high patio, they showed us bronze sculptures by Charlie Russell and other artists). Dorothy was working on the second of two volumes about their art collection and was interested in what we knew about Philip R. Goodwin. Her two books, *Harmsen's Western Americana* and *American Western Art* have since become standard reference books on American Western art. Together, they profile more than two hundred artists represented in the Harmsen collection, including Frederic Remington, Maynard Dixon, Herbert Dunton, William R. Leigh, Carl Rungius, and Georgia O'Keefe.

The art collection was Bill's idea. He had bought his first Western paintings in the late 1960s before prices for Western art skyrocketed. He'd rather buy paintings than collect stock certificates, he told us, because "they're a lot nicer to look at." Sometimes he would go into a gallery and buy a whole wall of them, he said. That way the dealer wouldn't know which painting he was really after. In less than a decade, their collection had grown to seven hundred paintings and sculptures. It filled the walls of their penthouse and the Jolly Rancher Candy plant in Golden.

My Harmsen article never made it to print, but I was paid $350 "upon acceptance" for the manuscript. (Many magazines pay only "upon publication"; you'll want to find out what to expect when talking terms.) I can't recall why *Americana* chose not to use the Harmsen piece, but this kind of thing happened sometimes. Another article I wrote for *Americana* concerning the restored commandant's residence at Fort Snelling in Minnesota was pulled when a fire destroyed the interior of the house. But if I was disappointed at not always seeing my work in print, I don't remember it. I was invariably busy with other projects, and besides, I had had the fun of, and learned from, doing the research and writing the articles.

In the beginning I sent finished articles off to editors, but I soon learned from *Writer's Market* that all that was typically needed was a query letter—to determine if an editor was even interested in my proposed subject or not. I learned how to write a good query letter, again from *Writer's Market*, and the response to my queries was usually positive. If I was asked to write on speculation, I would do so. I wouldn't have bothered to query the magazine unless I was quite certain that I could write a successful article. Within a couple of years I was writing on assignment for a half dozen magazines and occasionally for others.

Initially, I had stayed away from Twin Cities publications and editors, not wanting to have to explain my lack of academic credentials or experience. But I was developing a specialization in American history and art, and I was especially interested in *Minnesota* history and art. So after writing a fair number of articles for national magazines, which at least gave me experience, I began approaching local editors. One of the first people I called on was June Holmquist, who was head of publications at the Minnesota Historical Society in St. Paul.

I told June that I wanted to write for *Minnesota History*, the Historical Society's quarterly publication. *Minnesota History* did not usually pay for articles, but June arranged for me to receive a chairman's grant from the National

Endowment for the Humanities in the amount of four thousand dollars. My assignment was to write eight profiles of interesting Minnesota men and women in various walks of life for the magazine. I could choose my subjects.

The first person I profiled was Cream of Wheat artist Edward Brewer. By now I'd become intrigued with the whole Brewer family. Ed had shown me a copy of his father Nicholas Brewer's autobiography, *Trails of a Paintbrush* (Christopher House, 1938), and I'd been able to find my own copy in a second-hand bookshop. Nicholas Brewer was the son of a German immigrant who had headed west in the gold rush of 1849, found a bride in St. Louis before reaching California, and turned back. Eventually, following several years filled with hardships in different places, the Brewers settled in Olmsted County, Minnesota, where Nicholas was born in 1857. *Trails of a Paintbrush* chronicles his boyhood on the family farm in this lush Root River Valley country and his eventual rise to fame

Ed Brewer with painting for calendar

as one of this country's leading portrait painters. He also painted thousands of impressionistic landscapes that today bring good prices.

From *Trails of a Paintbrush*, I also learned more about Ed and his five brothers, two of whom, Reuben and Adrian, became painters as well. A third brother, Clarence, was adept at producing frames for "the Brewery." Referring to Ed in his book, Nicholas remarked, "It was useless to send him on an errand; he was sure to forget it and wander off chasing butterflies, poking after frogs, or robbing birds' nests." He also mentioned Ed's "predilection for drawing and sketching," adding, "He had a manner of scrawling his name at the top of his paper, saying, 'Well, I have to make my name first!'" When the time came, it was Nicholas who saw to it that Ed attended the Art Students' League in New York.

Ed Brewer's Cream of Wheat paintings reminded me of Norman Rockwell, and I compared him to the Vermont artist in my *Minnesota History* article. Like Rockwell, Brewer painted from his own surroundings, usually drawing his

"EMPTY, BY HECK!"

Painted by Edward V. Brewer for Cream of Wheat Co.   Copyright 1915 by Cream of Wheat Co.

ideas from simple and familiar things and experiences close to home. His zest for living enabled him to find inspiration in the commonest of everyday occurrences. "One morning," Brewer wrote (in "Composing an Advertising Illustration," an undated pamphlet which his daughter Barbara Brewer Peet showed me), "I entered the kitchen of our summer cottage with a fine bass for breakfast. My wife, in reaching for a package of breakfast food, discovered it to be empty." The idea was quickly transferred to canvas and appeared in the magazines as *Empty, By Heck!*

The Brewer article ran fourteen pages in *Minnesota History* and included twenty illustrations! Soon after it appeared in the Spring 1980 issue, editor

Ken Carley received a handwritten letter signed Dave Stivers on Nabisco letterhead:

> Dear Sir: Your Brewer article is very interesting. My compliments to Patricia Condon Johnston. Please let her know I dropped you a quick note. Hope we can meet someday. Please send five copies. $8.75 enclosed.

The next month Stivers announced the discovery of more than six hundred Cream of Wheat paintings, long thought destroyed, in a group of metal lockers in Cream of Wheat's Minneapolis plant. Nabisco put a value of one million dollars on the cache. Two years later, *Americana* magazine reported in its July/August 1982 issue that Stivers was organizing a Cream of Wheat art show that would travel to museums around the country. "These paintings are real Americana," Stivers was quoted as saying, "and should be seen." My sentiments exactly.

For my second *Minnesota History* subject, I chose St. Paul stereophotographer Truman W. Ingersoll (1862-1922). Ingersoll's son, Ward Ingersoll, had called and come to see Charlie and me after reading my Philip R. Goodwin article in *Persimmon Hill.* His father had collected Goodwin prints, Ward told us, and he wanted to introduce us to Truman Ingersoll and his work. Ward was then in his eighties and eager to perpetuate his father's reputation. He invited Charlie and me to his home in Ed Brewer's old neighborhood near the Town and Country Club in St. Paul.

Truman Ingersoll turned out to be a great story. In the years surrounding the turn of the century, the St. Paul photographer had pictured the world—or at least a good part of it. His specialty was stereophotography, and he marketed his staggering collection of stereoscopic views with uncommon success. That would have been enough, but his legacy also includes a perceptive portrait of late-nineteenth-century St. Paul, with particular emphasis on the high-spirited entertainments enjoyed by its better-heeled inhabitants.

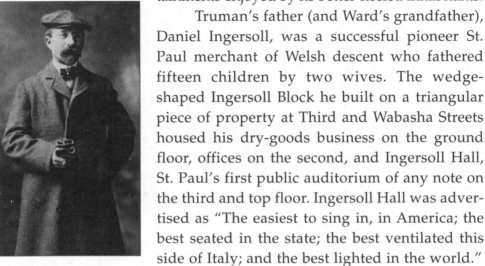

Truman W. Ingersoll

Truman's father (and Ward's grandfather), Daniel Ingersoll, was a successful pioneer St. Paul merchant of Welsh descent who fathered fifteen children by two wives. The wedge-shaped Ingersoll Block he built on a triangular piece of property at Third and Wabasha Streets housed his dry-goods business on the ground floor, offices on the second, and Ingersoll Hall, St. Paul's first public auditorium of any note on the third and top floor. Ingersoll Hall was advertised as "The easiest to sing in, in America; the best seated in the state; the best ventilated this side of Italy; and the best lighted in the world."

Young Truman grew up in a sizable frame house near Scott Fitzgerald's Summit Avenue, walked to classes at Jefferson Grade School (where my husband Charlie also went to school), lost an eye at an early age in an accident involving an arrow made from a corset stay (which made his later work in stereophotography all the more remarkable), and left home at seventeen to seek his fortune in the American West as a civil engineer, a career that lasted only two years.

After returning home to St. Paul and clerking briefly in his father's store, Truman turned to photography and was soon doing a land-office business in stereoscopic views. By 1884 his first commercial studio at 160 West Third Street was a paying proposition. Stereo viewing with a hand-held stereoscope was a national pastime, and for the next quarter century, while maintaining his family and business in St. Paul, Truman Ingersoll traveled the world in search of unusual pictures.

Ward showed us hundreds upon hundreds of his father's amazing stereo cards—an astonishing kaleidoscope of North American views that ranged from the Klondike to Mexico, including the Chicago World's Fair in 1893 and the San Francisco earthquake in 1906; European views, primarily those of Sweden and Norway; and pictures of Palestine, Greece, Italy (where he convinced Pope Pius X to pose for him), and Japan (which Truman termed "Nippon land").

At home in St. Paul, he was the "official" photographer for his society friends' outings and entertainments, which included sailing at White Bear Lake and automobile excursions. A 1907 newspaper article listed Ingersoll as one of sixteen drivers of "big touring cars" who drove "the ninety miles [from the Twin Cities to Mankato, Minnesota] without mishap of any kind." Some of his best-known photographs depict the splendiferous ice palaces constructed for early St. Paul winter carnivals, and he also captured the antics of the fun-loving Nushka Club, whose members dressed and paraded as "polar bears" during carnival festivities.

At its peak, the Ingersoll View Company employed some twenty-five workers, many of them young women who hand-tinted the photos. Technology eventually caught

up with the photographer, however, and public interest in stereo views waned. Moving pictures were the new rage when Truman Ingersoll retired from business in 1909. Packing up his

family, he moved to Buffalo Lake, Minnesota, where he developed a thriving whole-sale flower business. Ward Ingersoll remembered pack-ing gladioli in banana crates for shipment on the ten o'clock evening train. Once, he told me, the family sup-plied 65,000 live daisies for Dayton's (the Minneapolis department store) first "Daisy Sale."

Truman Ingersoll's studio at 88-92 West Fourth Street, the present site of the St. Paul Public Library

One especially nice aspect of writing these pro-files usually involved meeting the families of the "profilees." Family members typically provided all manner of materi-al—from family photographs and news clippings to their own recollections about the subject's life and values. Ward Ingersoll had provided much of the source material for my article about his father, and Ed Brewer's daughter, Barbara Brewer Peet (a third-generation Brewer family artist who also painted portraits), had spent several days with me sift-ing through boxes of letters and papers and photographs that had been salvaged when her father's studio burned shortly before his death in 1971.

Ellen Ireland, a pioneer St. Paul educator and adminis-trator, was the subject of my next *Minnesota History* profile, but this time there was no family nor any descendants. Ellen Ireland (1842-1930) had been a Sister of St. Joseph. Her religious name was Sister Seraphine. She was the sister of Archbishop John Ireland and his female counterpart. I was drawn to her story because I had graduated in the Ellen Ireland Auditorium at St. Joseph's Academy and wanted to know more about her. But I was also somewhat apprehensive about how difficult it might be to try to reconstruct her life.

Not only were there no family members who might be able to help me, there were no Ellen Ireland papers. Having embraced a life of penance and poverty, one sister of St. Joseph explained to me, nuns of her era were discouraged from keeping personal memorabilia including letters and photographs. The beginning of Lent was often a time for ridding oneself of this extraneous material, and what little remained was usually destroyed when a sister died.

But Ellen Ireland's life did not go unrecorded, and I was delighted to find a wealth of material awaiting me at the archives of the Sisters of St. Joseph at the College of St. Catherine in St. Paul. Many Roman Catholic nuns had

St. Joseph's Academy, where Ellen Ireland spent most of her life and where I later attended high school

changed their views of themselves and their roles over the past few decades, I learned. Several sisters of St. Joseph who saw the value in preserving the history of their order and the individual nuns had written about their community. A book by Sister Helen Angela Hurley, *On Good Ground: The Story of the Sisters of St. Joseph in St. Paul* (1951) provided a starting point. The archives yielded several biographical sketches of Ellen Ireland and a copy of her baptismal certificate from Ireland. More information was gleaned from both published and unpublished material about her brother Archbishop John Ireland.

Sister Ellen Ireland

The sisters welcomed me with open arms. I was the first person "from the outside" who had come in to do any serious work on their community, they told me. Sister Anne Thomasine Sampson, who had written about the order and also initiated an oral history project for the Sisters of St. Joseph, was especially helpful and shared her work with me. Several of her interviews with older nuns contained information about Ellen Ireland. I also interviewed sisters still living at the college who remembered her. The story that emerged about this amazing woman was richer than I had ever imagined.

Ellen Ireland had come with her large family to America when the potato famines drove them out of Ireland. She was ten years old when she enrolled at St. Joseph's Academy in St. Paul in 1852. After graduating six years later, she entered the convent, and at nineteen, she was appointed directress at the Academy. In the 1870s Sister Seraphine was sent with six other nuns to found a convent in Hastings, Minnesota, and from 1877 to 1882, she was superior at the

Catholic orphanage for girls in St. Paul's Lowertown. She was described as "being of a strong and robust constitution," and it was noted that she "usually bore the heaviest part of the burden and was first in the laundry, kitchen, and at the scrubbing."

When she was forty years old in 1882, Sister Seraphine was elected Mother Superior of the Sisters of St. Joseph's St. Paul Province, which embraced Minnesota and North and South Dakota. Under her direction during the next thirty-nine years (she was re-elected to her three-year term twelve times), the Sisters opened more than thirty new schools, often under extreme hardships, and established five hospitals. Ultimately, Mother Seraphine accomplished her dream of founding a college for women—the College of St. Catherine in St. Paul.

The first of Mother Seraphine's projects was St. Agatha's Conservatory of Music and Art in downtown St. Paul. Intended as a home for sisters who were teaching in downtown parochial schools (at one time it housed ninety sisters), it was also unique among the sisters' institutions. The income derived from art and music classes and other enterprises conducted there provided a much-needed revenue stream for the always hard-pressed community. In addition to teaching an astounding number of classes (a full-page advertisement in a Twin Cities musicians' directory for 1912-13 listed piano, organ, violin, zither, theory, history of music, harmony, mandolin, guitar, banjo, counterpoint, voice culture, elocution, languages, painting, china decorating, and drawing), the sisters at St. Agatha's were constantly at work painting and selling pictures or hand-painting and firing their popular chinaware. They also sold calendars door-to-door and, to help build St. Catherine's, peddled a special edition of Archbishop Ireland's sermons and addresses.

The need for money was constant but so was the need for young women to help carry on the expanding work of the community, and Mother Seraphine had a real talent for recruiting the latter. She had that rare personal quality called charisma and she was persistent. From the parishes where they taught, her sisters regularly brought girls to meet her. Once Mother Seraphine decided that a visitor had a vocation, the girl usually ended up joining the convent—whether she had originally had any intention of doing so or not.

I interviewed one elderly nun who told me that she had been twenty-one when she went with her fifteen-year-old sister to meet Mother Seraphine. The younger girl wanted to join the convent, but Mother Seraphine felt she was too young. "Then Mother Seraphine came over to me and patted me on the cheek—she always did that—and said, 'How old are you?' I told her, and she said, 'Well, you're the one who should come.'" This woman had been a sister of St. Joseph for seventy years in 1982.

Another girl, a serious music student at St. Agatha's in 1919, was taken to St. Joseph's Academy and left alone in a parlor with Mother Seraphine. It seemed like a chance meeting but it was doubtless otherwise. Mother Seraphine took an immediate interest in her, and before their conversation had progressed very far, said, "I think you have a vocation."

"Oh no, not now," the girl replied. "I might enter sometime, but *not now.*"

"What would keep you from entering now?" Mother wanted to know.

"Well, the biggest thing is that I am supposed to appear in a recital with Dr. [Silvio] Scionti in the spring. And that must be."

The conversation took another direction until Mother said, "I think you'd better enter in February. Why don't you consider this? If you enter the convent you can dress in secular clothes in the spring and send out invitations and put on this program just as you would have."

The girl was still quite sure she did not want to enter but promised to think about it. Their conversation continued at some length, she recalled, and then Mother dismissed her with a good pat on the cheek. "She'd always give you a loving pat on the cheek—and sometimes it wasn't so loving!" The meeting had its intended result. The girl entered the novitiate in February 1920. In 1982 she had been teaching music for the sisters for sixty-one years.

This nun was Sister Carlos Eue, my former piano teacher at St. Joseph's Academy. I enjoyed seeing her after so many years, and she wrote to me after my article appeared in *Minnesota History*:

> To relive my interview with dear Mother Seraphine Ireland brought back sacred memories indeed, even though I was a bit chagrined with the meeting at the time. These many years in religious life have been filled with much happiness and never for even a moment have I wanted to be any place else.

Many of the people I have profiled over the years have provided inspiration for my own life, and this was especially true of Ellen Ireland and the Sisters of St. Joseph. There is a lot to be learned from the example of religious women who find untold happiness in giving totally of themselves. There is a peace and serenity in their lives that I think we can partially duplicate on the "outside" by living according to high principles and by doing the work we have chosen to the best of our God-given abilities. I make a conscious effort every day to try to live my life this way.

4

Fitzgerald Fever

IN 1981 I STARTED writing for *Twin Cities* magazine and editor John Hodowanic. *Twin Cities* was a new and glamorous publication, and John was a real peach, savvy and smart, and open to almost anything I wanted to write about. My first article for the magazine was "All Dolled Up—and Stillwater's Her Name." Some editors like to write their own titles, and John was one of them. I liked it that he usually saved me the trouble of coming up with something catchy. "All Dolled Up" appeared in the April issue and would lead the next year to my first book.

My articles appeared in almost every issue after that. For May, I wrote "When the Saints Go Marching Into Mendota." Mendota was Minnesota's earliest white settlement, handily located at the confluence of the Mississippi and the Minnesota Rivers, where in 1835 fur trader Henry Sibley built his still extant two-story yellow limestone house, and began trading with the Indians. Sibley prospered and fathered a half-blood daughter by a Dakota woman before going on to become Minnesota's first governor in 1858. By then, the fur trade was petering out and Mendota along with it.

The down-on-its-luck town became a hangout for whiskey sellers and gamblers, and honky-tonk music found the place. By the late 1930s Mendota had a resident Dixieland band, and when they were playing clubs in the Twin Cities, big-name musicians including Hoagy Carmichael, Jack Teagarden, Gene Krupa, and Harry James came to jam at Mendota. Fast forward to the 1980s and the Hall Brothers Jazz Band was playing Dixieland music every Friday and Saturday night at the Emporium of Jazz. I loved the music, hated the heavy cigarette smoke in the place, but put up with it to listen to the Hall Brothers.

I was liking Minnesota history more and more all the time and having fun writing about it. Imagine doing research for an article by listening to the sweetest Dixieland north of New Orleans! This was just about as good as it gets, and the good times only got better.

For the June issue of *Twin Cities*, I wrote "The Moon Shines on Pretty Red Wing," which allowed me to spend several spring days in that idyllic community. Red Wing is a small Mississippi River city famous for its pottery and now home to the Red Wing Shoe Company and the refurbished St. James Hotel. The town grew up on the site of a village belonging to Dakota Indians who lived in

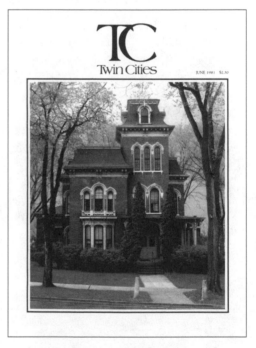

"Pretty Red Wing" was a cover story for Twin Cities *magazine.*

bark lodges and skin-covered cone-shaped tepees at the river's edge. Higher up, around the base of local landmark Barn Bluff, they tended fields of corn and squash. French traders in the mid-1700s called the chief at this village "L'Aile Rouge" (Red Wing) because he carried a swan's wing dyed scarlet as his talisman. In the 1980s, like Stillwater, Red Wing was in the midst of a well-planned revival to refurbish her Victorian image and increase her tourist appeal.

Tourists had come here early on. In 1861 Henry David Thoreau had traveled upriver to Red Wing. Minnesota was touted as a health resort, and Thoreau was ailing with tuberculosis. He opened his mail on Barn Bluff, made detailed lists of the local flora, and marveled at the "grandeur and beauty" of the Mississippi River Valley in this region. Unfortunately, the Minnesota climate did nothing for his health, and Thoreau died the next year at the age of forty-four.

Red Wing also had its own homegrown talent to rave about. Local resident and ethnomusicologist Frances Densmore

Frances Densmore

was one of the most remarkable women Minnesota has ever produced. At a time when most Americans of her generation were bent on eradicating Indian culture, Miss Densmore immersed herself in studying and preserving Indian music.

"I heard an Indian drum when I was very, very young," is how she explained her lifelong fascination. The Densmore home in Red Wing commanded a view of the Mississippi River, and on an island opposite the town there was a Dakota camp. "At night when they were dancing, we could hear the sound of the drum and see the flicker of their campfire," she remembered.

"I fell asleep with my mind full of fancies about the interesting people across the Mississippi."

By the time she died in Red Wing at ninety in 1957, Frances Densmore had made more than three thousand recordings of Indian music and published more than twenty books and two hundred articles on the subject.

Red Wing's other celebrity residents have included Alexander P. Anderson, the scientist who created Puffed Wheat and Puffed Rice; Dr. Charles N. Hewitt, the first physician to produce and use smallpox vaccine in Minnesota; and Eugenie Anderson, this country's first woman ambassador (whom President Truman once called "the finest human being I know.") Eugenie was Alexander Anderson's daughter-in-law. Another notable, West Point graduate Lauris Norstad, was the son of the pastor of St. Peter's Lutheran Church in Red Wing and went on to become Supreme Allied Commander in Europe of NATO during the Eisenhower administration.

In August 1981, I had two articles in *Twin Cities*, "Guarding the Colonel's Place in History" and "Gambling on Riverboats." The first was about Fort Snelling's troubled first commandant Josiah Snelling. Colonel Snelling was a heavy drinker who was facing a court martial at the time of his death at age forty-six from chronic diarrhea. Had he or had not he confused his personal accounts with those of the U.S. government? On the flip side of the coin, to his enduring credit, the magnificent yellow limestone fort he erected at the confluence of the Mississippi and Minnesota Rivers was the finest fort ever built in the American West. Today, within shouting distance of the Twin Cities Metropolitan Airport, Fort Snelling is a major Minnesota tourist attraction.

"Gambling on Riverboats" was the story of local entrepreneur Bill Bowell who had given up corporate life to operate his own fleet of vintage sternwheel steamboats up and down the Mississippi. Doing research for this piece was particularly pleasant: Captain Bowell treated Charlie (who did the photography for this piece) and me to a day trip on the river. Some of my subsequent pieces for *Twin Cities* were titled "Didn't We Meet on Madeline Island?" (a wonderfully historic resort island in Lake Superior), "No Bull About James J. Hill's Model Farm (which was later developed as the exclusive present-day St. Paul suburb of North Oaks), and "The Magic of Dr. Charlie's Mayowood" (the Mayo home in Rochester, now open to the public).

I never ran out of fascinating Minnesota material to write about for *Twin Cities.* Some subjects I found close to home in Afton. I wrote about our neighbors' horses ("My Kingdom For A Horse—Provided It's A Morgan") and our local Afton Toy

General John Henry Hammond

Shop ("Yes, We have No Electric Trains"). One of my favorites pieces, which appeared in the May 1982 issue, was titled "St. Paul History in a Roll-top Desk."

In 1953 a packet of papers containing a previously unknown journal by William Henry Clark had turned up in a St. Paul attic. The papers had been in the possession of General John Henry Hammond, who had been General Sherman's chief of staff during the Civil War. Following the war, General Hammond moved his family to St. Paul, where they lived for a time in the house that is now Forepaugh's restaurant at 276 South Exchange Street. Their nearest neighbor across the street was Governor Alexander Ramsey. General Hammond engaged in railroad building and actively promoted the development of the Duluth-Superior area. One of his partners was James J. Hill.

The Clark papers were found in a house at 117 Farrington Avenue that had belonged to General Hammond's daughter, Mrs. Sophia Hammond Foster. Following Mrs. Foster's death in late 1952, her daughter, Mrs. Vaclav Vytlacil, had come to St. Paul to dispose of the house and its belongings. Remembering that her mother had once remarked that the papers contained in her grandfather's desk might have some historical value, Mrs. Vytlacil asked the Minnesota Historical Society to look them over and select what it wanted.

Minnesota Historical Society curator Lucile Kane found the Clark papers in this Hammond family desk.

As it turned out, the general's papers included an original portion of perhaps the most important narrative of North American exploration ever written—a partial record of the Lewis and Clark expedition of 1803–06! The *St. Paul Dispatch* called the find the "greatest discovery of its kind in decades."

The national wire services picked up the story of the "priceless collection," *Time* and *Life* sent reporters to St. Paul, and the Historical Society was besieged with calls and telegrams from publishers throughout the country. The publicity also touched off a six-year, three-way legal tussle to determine the papers' rightful owners. Several of General Hammond's heirs contested the gift to the Minnesota Historical Society, and the U.S. government also laid claim to the papers, maintaining that Clark had created them in the course of his official duty as a federal employee.

To write this story, I interviewed some of the principals in the case including Lucile Kane, who was curator of manuscripts at the Minnesota Historical Society when the papers were discovered. Lucile was the one who had actually gone to the Farrington Avenue house and carried the papers back to the Historical Society. I also found additional material in Minnesota Historical Society files including numerous newspaper articles detailing the spectacular find and the ensuing legal contest.

So how did the lawsuit come out? The heirs won and later sold the manuscripts to Yale University. The question of how General Hammond had obtained the Clark papers was never fully answered.

The government contended that he may have obtained them illegally. In 1878 Hammond had been appointed Dakota Superintendent of Indian Affairs and ordered to Lawrence, Kansas, to shut down the Central Superintendency of Indian Affairs. This office had formerly been located at St. Louis and headed by William Clark from 1807 until his death in 1838. Hammond may have taken possession of the Clark papers while closing the Indian Affairs office. There was no proof of this, however, and Judge Gunnar Nordbye, when he handed down his decision nine months following the four-day trial, stated that the government had not sustained the burden of proof in establishing its claim to the material.

Another of my articles, for the October 1982 issue of *Twin Cities*, was about Scott and Zelda Fitzgerald. Minneapolis and St. Paul were in the grip of Fitzgerald fever, with three large Fitzgerald events in the offing: an original play by local playwright Lance Belville titled *Scott and Zelda: The Beautiful Fools* was set to open at the Landmark Center in St. Paul; the St. Paul Public Library was celebrating its 100th birthday with a series of programs called "F. Scott Fitzgerald Revisited"; and the University of Minnesota was planning a national Fitzgerald conference.

What more could possibly be said about this famous couple, I wondered. Since Fitzgerald's early death in 1940, more than forty books and many hundreds of articles had been written about the St. Paul author.

But wait. Enter local Fitzgerald scholar Lloyd Hackl, who had been quietly putting together a collection of materials including letters and photographs that would wind up at the Minnesota Historical Society. Hackl had located a number of people in St. Paul and the White Bear area who had known the Fitzgeralds and gained entrance to most of their homes. Alexander "Xandra" Kalman, for instance, with her husband, Oscar, had been among the Fitzgeralds' closest friends.

Xandra had grown up in St. Paul with Scott and enrolled with him in Professor Baker's dancing classes at Ramaley Hall on Grand Avenue. After Scott and Zelda returned to St. Paul for their daughter Scottie's birth in 1921, Xandra found a house for them at 626 Goodrich that belonged to rel-

Scott and Zelda Fitzgerald, a month before their daughter, Scottie, was born

atives of hers. (This is where Scott revised the proofs for *The Beautiful and Damned*, which Scribner's published in April 1922). The next summer when the Fitzgeralds moved out to the White Bear Yacht Club, Xandra and Zelda played golf while Scott spent his days writing. "We dubbed around," Xandra recalled. "Neither one of us was any good at golf."

The Kalmans were with the Fitzgeralds in Paris in 1930 when Zelda suffered her first breakdown. They had been dining together, Xandra remembered, when Zelda abruptly got up from the table to hurry to a dancing lesson. Seeing how nervous she was, Oscar Kalman went along with her. She changed into her dancing clothes in the taxi with Kalman telling her that she was pushing herself too hard, but she seemed not to hear him. When the car stopped at a crossing, she jumped out and ran toward her studio. Kalman was seriously concerned that there might be something wrong with Zelda, he told Scott afterwards. Later that month Zelda was hospitalized at Malmaison on the outskirts of Paris.

Mrs. Kalman owned several paintings Zelda made while she was convalescing in the 1930s. Much of the time Zelda painted flowers or fanciful landscapes, but one of the paintings pictured a group of ballet dancers as they would *feel* after a strenuous rehearsal. A cleverly conceived piece, almost reminiscent of Picasso, its figures are depicted with painfully enlarged and contorted muscles.

Mrs. Kalman also had a thick file of correspondence between her husband and the Fitzgeralds that turned up in Kalman's office after his death. In one letter, Fitzgerald tells Kalman that his story "Winter Dreams" was about "you and Xandra." Kalman replied that he had read the piece but failed to see any resemblance between its characters and his wife and himself.

The primary reason for Scott's letters, though, was that he needed money. His mother Mollie Fitzgerald had died recently (in September 1936), leaving an estate of approximately $45,000 to be divided between Scott and his sister Annabel. Scott couldn't wait the six months it would take for the estate to be settled, however. (His income reached an all-time low in 1936—$10,180, and he was in poor health.) In the meantime, he borrowed $7,500 from Kalman.

There were also eleven handwritten letters to Kalman—"Kollie," as she called him—from Zelda. These dated from the 1940s, after Zelda had returned to live with her mother on Sayre Street in Montgomery, Alabama. The first of them thanks Kalman for his concern for her following Scott's death (Fitzgerald died of a heart attack on December 21, 1940). Scott loved his friends deeply, she told him, and the two had always hoped to repay the many kindnesses shown them. "Now that he won't be coming East again, with his pockets full of promises and his notebook full of schemes, and new refurbished hopes, life doesn't offer as happy a vista," she wrote.

The handwriting in Zelda's letters varied considerably. She would continue to suffer periods of emotional instability until her own death in a fire in the hospital where she was a patient in 1948. She became intensely concerned with the salvation of her soul during these later years and mentions the subject in several of the letters. In one, she also asks Kalman for a loan of seventy-five dollars.

Scottie was coming to see her during the summer of 1945, and she wanted the money to buy a woman's membership in the local country club. Montgomery was a perfectly marvelous old city, but there was absolutely nothing to do there—no theater or gay restaurants or anything of the kind, she explained. She was hesitant to bother Kalman about the matter, she said, but "my family would, surely, not lend me the money for such a purpose as they sometimes send me wool underwear for Christmas if you see what I mean." She also wanted him to understand that she wasn't asking for the money for herself—that she only wanted Scottie to have a good time.

Lloyd Hackl also talked with Betty Binger, the daughter of one of Fitzgerald's childhood sweethearts, Elizabeth "Litz" Clarkson. Mrs. Binger had letters Scott had written to her mother in 1915 when he was at Princeton. "Remember Litz," he says in one of them, "until we meet 'when the Holly blooms' in three months you are 'She who (Quick somebody. Give me an appropriate quotashun) well anyway you are she who." Mrs. Binger called Hackl one day to say that she had found a roll of undeveloped film from 1914. She had had the pictures finished and several of them included Fitzgerald.

I was having the time of my life, of course. These were truly "golden years" when I was writing for John Hodowanic and *Twin Cities* magazine (which, unfortunately, eventually disappeared from the Twin Cities publishing scene). John would write me wonderfully funny letters when I had submitted something he especially liked. He made writing for magazines seem very glamorous, and it *was* when you were writing for John. He made you feel special, he was fair, and editor/author lunches were sometimes part of the package. For me, it was like New York, which I had never experienced, in Minneapolis.

During the early 1980s I was also still writing for *The American West*. One article titled "N. C. Wyeth and Cream of Wheat" revisited Cream of Wheat ads. This was a short piece—just two pages with illustrations of the two Minneapolis Institute of Arts paintings—that was appended to an article by another writer about a traveling exhibition of Wyeth paintings that was opening at the Buffalo Bill Historical Center in Cody, Wyoming. *The American West* magazine, too, was in its heyday in the 1980s, with interesting articles, good writing, and splashy layouts.

Another *American West* article of mine about Taos painter W. Herbert "Buck" Dunton was based on an unpublished

Where the Mail Goes, Cream of Wheat Goes
by N. C. Wyeth

biography of the artist by his son, Ivan Dunton. Charlie and I had met Ivan Dunton on a trip west and still have and treasure a small oil sketch of his father's that we purchased from him. There had been cartons of similar on-location landscape sketches in Buck's studio when he died, Ivan said, along with instructions to destroy all of them. He and his sister had built a bonfire and were already burning the sketches when they decided to call a halt to the destruction. Our sketch was one of the ones they rescued.

During the early years of this century, Buck Dunton was a busy and successful New York illustrator. His output was voluminous—he supplied artwork to some twenty magazines and illustrated forty-nine books—and his income reflected his success. By the time he was thirty, Dunton was a wealthy man. Then, at the peak of his career, he quit New York to move to Taos where he could devote his whole time and enthusiasm to painting "fine art."

His money ran out, and he was never again well-to-do. His wife couldn't endure the primitive living conditions in New Mexico, and his marriage ended in a permanent separation. But Buck Dunton remained completely committed to serious painting and needed little to satisfy himself. "I have learned to live with my own mind," he told the press,

W. HERBERT DUNTON:
HE DEVOTED A LIFETIME TO PAINTING THE REAL WEST
BY PATRICIA CONDON JOHNSTON

"to have few material wants, to enjoy myself in the open—or with a good book. I believe I have found the secret of contentment, which is the work I love and the enjoyment of simple things."

Spreading my growing interest in American art around, I wrote about Henry Lewis, whose work I had seen at the Minnesota Historical Society, for *American History Illustrated*. Lewis was an American artist, born in England, who trained in Dusseldorf. In the 1840s he began work on a mammoth panorama of the Mississippi River Valley, twelve feet high by thirteen hundred yards long, rolled on cylinders, with which he hoped to make his fortune. He didn't, but he went on to produce an illustrated reader that was the finest book of its kind ever published. Designed to promote immigration to the Mississippi Valley, *Das illustrirte Mississippithal* (published in Dusseldorf in twenty parts between 1854 and 1857) was a valuable geography of the area, from the Falls of St. Anthony to the Gulf of Mexico. Lewis's seventy-eight color plates made it a masterwork.

Timberline *by W. Herbert Dunton*

Cowgirl with Red Scarf *by W. Herbert Dunton*

American History Illustrated also published a short piece of mine about Coles Phillips, a popular New York illustrator during the early years of this century who achieved uncanny success with his trademark "Fade-Away Girls." I'd started looking into this artist after seeing some of his old prints in a friend's kitchen. So as not to overdose on artists, I also wrote a piece for *AHI* titled "Early American Bookplates." My interest in bookplates was prompted by a heavy, nineteenth-century book about them I had picked up in a used bookstore.

A "fade-away" girl by Coles Phillips

IF MY EARLY EXPERIENCE in writing for publication sounds too good to be true, it seemed that way to me too. I felt lucky beyond reason. I'm not a highly creative writer, but I had caught on to some of the basics of writing for magazines.

The single most important piece of advice I can give to beginning writers is to learn to match your subject matter with the appropriate magazine. *This is absolutely critical*, and it was, I believe, the secret of my success. It was the first and foremost reason I was able to sell my first magazine article. Cream of Wheat ads was a great fit for *Americana* magazine.

You can't write a magazine article without a particular publication in mind and then hope to sell it. It doesn't usually work that way. You need to shape your article or query for a specific magazine. Read *Writer's Market* and familiarize yourself with magazines that publish the kind of subject matter that interests you. Many publications will be glad to send you their "writers' guidelines." These typically outline what kind of articles the magazine is looking for and how to go about presenting your material to them.

Secondly, you need to have a passionate interest in your material that leads you to explore it fully. I always wrote articles about subjects that I wanted to research and know more about. You will want to choose interesting subject material, of course, but almost any topic can be made interesting. It's all in how you present it: witness my early articles about apples and lilacs. If prosaic subjects such as these can be winners, think what you can do with more exotic material!

Ideas for articles are all around you. I've just opened a 1980s *Americana* magazine to a fascinating article about one-of-a-kind gravestones in the Piedmont section of North Carolina. If I were in the market for an idea for an article, I'd consider one about tombstones in our neck of the woods. Red pottery grave markers are common in and around Red Wing, Minnesota, for instance, where the town's first sewer pipes were also made of the same, plentiful red clay.

It also goes without saying that you will do the best job you possibly can of researching and writing your article and collecting illustrations. Many of my articles relied on great artwork including paintings and photographs. There are many sources for illustrations including museums, historical societies, and local photographers. In my case, of course, Charlie often provided untold help in the illustration department.

Whenever an editor suggested changes or additions, I made them gladly. I valued this on-the-job training and made a point of developing good working relationships with magazine editors. I was learning how to succeed at writing for publication from them, and many of them suggested additional articles to me. I also, and this is important, *always* met deadlines. Besides giving each article my best, I always made sure it arrived on an editor's desk by the agreed-upon due date.

I put in a lot of hours each day at my typewriter, so many that I sometimes got to feeling housebound. I had been writing for magazines for five years when I decided that it might be fun to work part-time in a bookstore. What could be more perfect? Working in a bookstore would get me out into the world among people and would also keep me stimulated. Charlie and I were doing a lot of "booking" each week at Odegard's Bookstore at Grand and Victoria in St. Paul (a few blocks from where I grew up), so one evening I approached owner Michele Poire Odegard. Michele and her co-owner husband Dan Odegard had done a really nice job of putting together a well-stocked independent bookstore.

Michele asked me to fill out an application, and I listed my magazine experience, thinking that this would probably impress her. It didn't. What Michele picked up on was my lack of schooling beyond high school. She was sorry, she said, but Odegard's preferred salespeople with at least some college. I remember being very disappointed, but the feeling didn't last. I was busy with a new writing project at home—my first book. I still felt insecure about my meager education, but I wasn't ready to tackle college. Not yet.

5

Minnesota's Earliest Whoopee-Town

THE STILLWATER ARTICLE for *Twin Cities* was a jumping off point for me. I'd never thought about writing a book before. Now the idea took hold of me and wouldn't let go. Delving into Stillwater's past felt like mining a precious commodity to me. I became preoccupied with this wonderfully historic river town a few miles upriver from Afton. Cashing in on her gaudy past, Stillwater in the 1980s was in the midst of a new boom that had everything to do with nostalgia. "Her history is suddenly her most valuable asset, her extravagant period architecture her trump card," I wrote for *Twin Cities*.

Historic signposts on both the north and south ends of Stillwater's Main Street welcome visitors to "The Birthplace of Minnesota." In 1848 Stillwater was the site of a convention of independence-minded citizens—mainly Yankee loggers and traders including future governor Henry Sibley—who successfully lobbied Congress for territorial status for Minnesota. Overnight, Stillwater became the capital city of lumbering on the St. Croix.

Author Stewart Holbrook called Stillwater "Minnesota's earliest whoopee-town." Come springtime, when the lumberjacks descended on Stillwater after six months' confinement in the northern camps, decent folks locked their doors. Whiskey

Lumberjacks on the St. Croix River in 1896, John Runk Collection

ran freely in the town's dozen saloons while the men warmed up to their freedom, proving their prowess with their fists. Some went on days-long drunken binges, "a sort of jollification," one reporter called it. Others hightailed it across the river to take their pleasure in the "sinkholes of sin" at St. Petersburgh (now Houlton, Wisconsin)—bordellos run by the likes of Red Nell and Perry the Pimp that relied on the Stillwater jacks to keep them in business.

The railroads reached Stillwater following the Civil War and more than a few fortunes were made. Young Stillwater came of age in the finest attire the lumbermen could afford. Men who made their money cutting and marketing timber flaunted it in their homes. Village forefathers had patterned their white-painted pine houses after those they remembered from the East, and the city came to look much like a typical New England town. Even so, few of the European-inspired architectual fads to change the face of America during the last century bypassed Stillwater. Pattern books provided local carpenters with all the details they needed to concoct a plethora of picturesque and exotic designs.

Heavily bracketed, squat Italian villas went up next to tall, white pine Gothic houses dripping medieval trimmings. Circumspect hip-roofed Federal homes were overshadowed by grandiloquent French imperial styles with more fashionable mansard roofs. Already elaborate facades were further embellished with cupolas and campaniles, turrets and tracery. The results of this architectural stew were quite eye-catching, and Stillwater remains a veritable museum of the delightful distractions of nineteenth-century architecture.

The boom town was also a prison town. Stillwater had been passed over for state capital but awarded another prize of sorts: the state penitentiary. Congress appropriated twenty thousand dollars for the facility—considered a necessity in a new territory—and a three-story stone prison house with two "dungeons" was built in Battle Hollow, the site of a bloody encounter fourteen years earlier between the Dakota and the Ojibwe. Until 1921 inmates wore wool hip jackets, trousers, and skull caps with alternating black-and-white horizontal stripes.

The Minnesota State Prison on North Main Street in Stillwater, John Runk Collection

The prison's most notorious inmates were the three Younger brothers—Bob, James, and Cole—all of whom received

A prison official,
John Runk Collection

life sentences in 1876 for taking part in the attempted robbery of the First National Bank of Northfield, Minnesota, and the murder of cashier Joseph L. Heywood.

Stillwater's boom era couldn't last. It took burly loggers little more than fifty years to strip Minnesota's centuries-old pine forests. By the early years of this century, Stillwater was a has-been, choking on its own sawdust, while lumbermen turned their sights to the Pacific Northwest. In 1914, with all the "oldtimers" present, the last log was officially floated through the St. Croix boom. Stillwater thereafter went into a sharp decline that most residents assumed to be permanent.

But in recent decades Stillwater has made an amazing recovery. Improved highway access to the Twin Cities began attracting commuters. Then the preservationists got organized. The city stopped tearing down its old buildings and started sandblasting and revamping its period architecture. Street upon street of picturesque "painted ladies" now climb the steep river banks. The tourists started coming in droves.

I would never have considered a book, however, had it not been for the John Runk Collection of photographs. This is a truly spectacular trove that I discovered while working on the *Twin Cities* article. John Runk was a bachelor photographer who spent his lifetime picturing Stillwater. She was his favorite subject. In addition to his own photographs, made over a period of sixty-five years (1899-1964), he also collected pictures from earlier photographers, so that the Runk Collection spans one hundred years of Stillwater's

history. Few cities have had such colorful yesteryears as Stillwater. Fewer still
can boast a hometown photographer who
so faithfully preserved them.

In 1937 Runk donated a collection
of 435 photographs to Stillwater's Carnegie
Library. He presented them in asbestos-
lined metal cases that he had designed
himself to last "hundreds of years." After
his death in 1964, the bulk of his photographs—more than two thousand pictures—along with his glass-plate negatives, went to the Minnesota Historical
Society. Few of his myriad views of
Stillwater had ever been published. Nor

*John Runk in a promotional
photo for his American
Eagle Studio*

had anyone ever written a book about Stillwater (although
several early St. Croix Valley histories included accounts of
the community). The more I poked about in Stillwater's past,
the more convinced I became that I should write a popular
history that would showcase the Runk photographs.

*John Runk, on the left, was also
a keen outdoorsman.*

Could I actually write
a book? I wouldn't know
unless I tried, but I thought
that I probably could. I
wasn't having any trouble
writing for magazines, and
a Stillwater book would be
largely a matter of flesh-
ing out what I had already
written for *Twin Cities*. I
began by going back and
wresting more detail from
the research materials I'd

used. These included James Taylor Dunn's *The St. Croix: Midwest Border River* (1965), the best (and only comprehensive) popular history of the St. Croix Valley, W. H. C. Folsom's *Fifty Years in the Northwest* (1888), Augustus B. Easton's two volume *History of the St. Croix Valley* (1909), and Rev. Neill's *History of Washington County and the St. Croix Valley* (1881). By this time, I had added these books to my home library.

Charlie and I used to spend most of our Saturdays browsing new and used bookshops. I've always tried to buy as many of the books that I use as possible, and I have accumulated good collections of Minnesota history and American art history books. Sometimes I buy two copies of the same book. I have a boxed, signed limited edition of the James Taylor Dunn book, for instance, and also what I call a working copy, which has seen a lot of use.

Librarian Sue Collins at the Stillwater Public Library was a great booster for my book project and enormously helpful. I spent countless pleasant hours in the library's downstairs Minnesota Room, working in its well-organized newspaper clippings file. Sue had taped a series of oral history interviews with longtime Stillwater residents that helped fill in gaps. She also introduced me to Stillwater residents who shared their family reminiscences and personal research with me. Local history buff Diane Thompson sent me home with armloads of material she had compiled about Yankee lumberman Isaac Staples, the town's godfather if you will, whose palatial Italianate residence on Stillwater's North Hill overlooked his riverfront sawmill.

By early 1982 I had completed a manuscript of about 30,000 words for a book titled *Stillwater: Minnesota's Birthplace in photographs by John Runk*. This was really quite a feat for me. My magazine pieces were usually 1,500-2,500 words, although the profiles for *Minnesota History* averaged about 5,000 words. Charlie photographed a hundred or so of the Runk photographs at the Stillwater Library and the Minnesota Historical Society, and both institutions gave us permission to reproduce them. With manuscript and photos in hand, now all I had to do was to find a publisher. If only it had been that simple.

Isaac Staples riverfront domain, John Runk Collection

Dorn Communications, which published *Twin Cities*, had a book division, so I presented *Stillwater* to the editor there first, pointing up its wonderful John Runk photos. Wouldn't he be interested in publishing this first history of Stillwater with its first-rate photographs?

Not at the present time, he replied noncommittally and with less enthusiasm than I would have liked. But he might consider it sometime in the future.

When a second publisher in Minneapolis told me much the same thing, I began to realize that finding a publisher might not be so easy.

Right about this time, fortunately, I was having lunch with an assistant editor from *Twin Cities* concerning an upcoming article, and I mentioned the Stillwater book to him. He suggested that I publish it myself. He told me about a newspaper editor he knew in Leavenworth, Kansas, who had published a book about Leavenworth and built himself a lake home with the profits. Leavenworth and Stillwater were much alike, he pointed out. Both had been rowdy lumber towns, both were prison towns, and both were lately catching on with tourists. If this newspaper man could publish his own book, my editor friend suggested, I could probably self-publish mine. I went home on wings.

Charlie liked the idea as well. Book lover and collector that he is, he wouldn't mind publishing a book, he said. We would need someone to design and produce it, and Charlie suggested Dale Johnston, one of his former art school class-mates and a successful graphic designer. When Dale said yes, we formed an informal partnership with him (that we later incorporated on the same day that we picked up the first copies of *Stillwater: Minnesota's Birthplace* from the bindery).

This was the beginning of Johnston Publishing, Inc. (we weren't blood-related, but we all shared the same Scottish surname), a joint venture in which Dale was an equal partner with Charlie and me. Dale made a gorgeous mockup of our intended book with a photograph of a turn-of-the-century balloon launching on the cover, and I began calling on Stillwater retailers. After getting bids from local printers, we decided to print 5,000 softcover copies—8" x 9" in a hori-zontal format with 96 pages—that would retail for $9.95. Dale thought we should pre-sell a certain number of the books before printing them, and that number (for reasons that now elude me) became 900. I could do it, I knew I could, and we set a press date.

I am a good salesperson when I need to be. Brick Alley Books on Main Street signed up for fifty copies. A second book-store ordered twenty-five, and Tamarack House art gallery want-ed two dozen. Carl Meister's German Band was pictured in the book, so I called on Carl's grandson, Tom Meister, who operated a saloon on Main Street. He took thirty-six to sell to patrons. Tom's cousin, Jon Meister, ran a garage in nearby Bayport. He called to say he wanted five copies. The Lowell Inn ordered one hundred copies to place in guest rooms and also to sell in the lobby. These were some of the easier sales.

Carl Meister's German Band in 1936

Bookstores in St. Paul and Minneapolis were more cautious, generally ordering five or ten copies, although Odegard Books in St. Paul (where I couldn't get a part-time job the year before) ordered twenty-five. Minnesota libraries gave me purchase orders, and Charlie and I took a day-trip to southern Minnesota where I called on bookstores and gift stores in Red Wing and Rochester. The two of us also went to see The Bookmen in Minneapolis. The Bookmen is a wholesaler that supplies books to libraries and retailers including the chain bookstores (which will almost never do business with a small publisher).

Bookmen partner Ned Waldman told Charlie and me that very rarely, maybe once in a hundred times, did he buy a book that "comes in off the street." But he was willing to look at what we had, and he ended up giving me an initial order for one hundred copies of *Stillwater*. We offered bookstores and other retailers a 40% discount off the retail price. Bookmen's terms as a wholesaler included a 50% discount, and the books were returnable if they didn't sell. By the date we were scheduled to begin printing, counting the Bookmen order, we had sold exactly 900 copies!

We contracted with the old North Central Publishing

Company in St. Paul to print the books and then discovered that we had misread the firm's bid. The stated price per copy for 5,000 softcover books—upon which we had based our retail price of $9.95—was contingent upon us also taking 1,000 hardcover books at a much higher price. We had thought the hardcover books were an option, but I was glad to have them. These clothbound books became a signed and numbered limited edition that we priced at $25. This seemed a lot then, but we ended up selling the last dozen or so of these books to a rare book dealer a few years ago for $45 apiece.

It cost approximately $20,000 to print and bind 5,000 softcover and 1,000 clothbound copies of *Stillwater: Minnesota's Birthplace.* I borrowed Charlie's and my share of the money from our family banker. I actually only had to borrow $6,600. By the time the printer's bill was due, thirty days after delivery, we had already collected several thousand dollars from retailers and others. We broke even on the *Stillwater* book in just six months.

We stored the books in our garage, letting our cars stand outside. Charlie and I delivered books to the stores and to Bookmen. The bindery had packed them in large boxes that were too heavy for either of us to lift, and we have ever since asked that our books be packed in cartons not to exceed thirty pounds. Librarian Sue Collins organized my first book signing at the Stillwater Public Library—a very nice affair with flowers and refreshments provided by friends of the library.

Our new book was front-page news in Stillwater— "Afton Author Tells Story of Stillwater With Runk Photos." I also took a copy to book reviewer Mary Ann Grossmann at the *St. Paul Pioneer Press Dispatch.* Mary Ann promised to look at it but told me that the paper didn't review self-published books as a matter of policy. "Have you seen this?" she asked, and she showed me a copy of a self-published novel by a local man. The man had put a lot of money into printing it, but most booksellers agreed that it was poorly written. A few days later, however, Mary Ann ran a photo from *Stillwater: Minnesota's Birthplace* in her books column along with information on how to order a copy from Johnston Publishing.

*In my home library, where
I wrote Stillwater book*

I sent another copy to the producer of the (Charlie) Boone and (Roger) Erickson radio show on WCCO in Minneapolis. Charlie Boone interviewed me on the air, and I remember him kidding me about the book being dedicated to him. (It was dedicated to my husband Charlie.) This was my first radio interview for one of my books, and I was nervous in the extreme. For the most part, I responded to Charlie's questions with a yes or no. I was also good at remembering exact dates. My family said that I sounded like a student in a classroom.

Some of the best publicity we received was completely unexpected. I had sent a copy of the book to editor Michael Durham in New York and enclosed a short note thanking him for having purchased my first magazine article. It hadn't occurred to me that he might be interested in excerpting from the book for *Americana*. When he called to ask if this was possible, I was stunned and stumbled through the conversation as best I could. Even after several years of working with editors, a call from one, especially one in New York, would still literally take my breath away.

(To explain my shortness of breath, I would sometimes say that I had just run in from out-of-doors, or that I had run up from the basement where I was doing laundry.)

The March/April 1983 issue of *Americana* carried a four-page portfolio of photographs from the book and ordering information. It was too much to believe that our first book was receiving national attention! We filled orders from all over the country—from people who had family ties to Stillwater, from steamboat aficionados (Runk photographed many of the hundreds of steamboats that had plied the St. Croix), from photography buffs.

Dale and Charlie and I had only intended to produce one book, but we hardly had *Stillwater* in the bookstores before I knew that we would continue publishing. Having once tasted of the heady elixir of self-publishing, I, for one, was having too much fun to stop with a single book. So

what next? Charlie had the answer. He was particularly interested in an article I was writing for *American History Illustrated* about a group of thirty-five paintings of Ojibwe Indians by American artist Eastman Johnson. The paintings were the most important collection owned by the St. Louis County Historical Society. They would make for a great little book, Charlie said.

I thought so too. Eastman Johnson (1824-1906) was the most celebrated American genre painter of his era. Lionized during the 1860s and 1870s for his sensitive paintings of country life, his subjects were common-

Charcoal and crayon sketches by Eastman Johnson

ly haymakers and cornhuskers, cranberry pickers and maple sugar makers. Less well-known was this series of paintings and drawings made earlier in his career of the native Ojibwe at Lake Superior. Working during 1856 and 1857 at Pokegama Bay and Grand Portage, Johnson painted individual portraits and group scenes as well as landscapes depicting Grand Portage, an important early fur-trading center.

The Johnson paintings rank with the finest examples of Indians in art in the nineteenth century, yet there is no indication that the artist ever exhibited them. Following his death in New York in 1906, his widow showed them at the American Museum of Natural History in New York. There they were seen by wealthy elevator manufacturer Richard Teller Crane who purchased them along with Indian apparel Johnson had used in the paintings and presented the entire collection to the city of Duluth. By the time Charlie and I saw them in the early 1980s, the paintings had been refurbished and placed on permanent display at the Depot Museum in Duluth. St. Louis County Historical Society Director Lawrence Sommer agreed to provide photographs of the paintings for a book and also gave me access to files concerning them.

Eastman Johnson's Lake Superior Indians was a tiny gem in hardcover, seven inches square, only seventy-two pages. We priced it to retail for $12.95 and printed 5,000 copies. Before sending the book to the printer, Charlie and I made a trip to Duluth one fine day to sell Larry Sommer on the idea of purchasing copies for the St. Louis County Historical Society to sell in their gift shop. I thought that I could probably sell him 1,000 copies at our usual 40% discount. On the drive up, I got to feeling even more optimistic. I could probably sell him 2,000 copies at a 50% discount, I told Charlie. Charlie didn't think so.

When I tried the 2,000 figure on Larry Sommer, however, he didn't blanch. He was definitely interested. "Just a minute,"

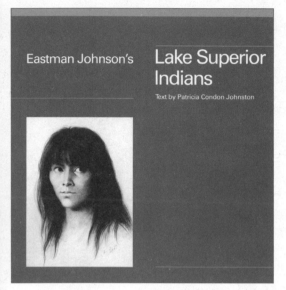

Eastman Johnson's **Lake Superior Indians**

Text by Patricia Condon Johnston

he said, and he got up and went out of the room we were in and returned with a padded mailing envelope. The Historical Society had quite a lot of these envelopes, he said, and he wanted to see if they would fit the book. The envelope fit. Perfectly. Larry gave us an order for 2,000 books. The three of us celebrated with lunch at a waterfront restaurant.

My article about Eastman Johnson in *American History Illustrated* (eight full pages with photographs of eight paintings) was terrific advance publicity for this small book, which received favorable notices in the *St. Paul Pioneer Press Dispatch*, the *Minneapolis Tribune*, the *St. Paul Downtowner*, *Inland Seas* (the quarterly journal of the Great Lakes Historical Society), *Minnesota Reviews*, the *St. Croix Valley Press*, the *Star Observer* (Hudson, Wisconsin), the *Duluth News-Tribune & Herald*, and *Encounters* magazine (published by the Science Museum of Minnesota).

Minnesota History magazine treated the book less kindly in a review by Minnesota Historical Society art curator Thomas O'Sullivan: "Unfortunately, author Patricia Condon Johnston has too little to say on the subject to fulfill the potential of this otherwise well-designed and illustrated volume," he complained. "The Eastman Johnson collection is a well-executed record of early Minnesota by a major American artist. It deserves deeper and more detailed treatment."

I couldn't believe that the Historical Society had done this to me! I sent Tom O'Sullivan a stiff letter. "*Eastman Johnson's Lake Superior Indians* was never intended as more than a brief introduction to a hitherto-little-known but spectacular

Minnesota collection," I bristled. "What I have been able to do is focus national attention on these paintings and drawings."

Tom wrote back to me that he stood by what he had written: "I think we at the Society best serve the public interests when we offer our sincere opinions."

Tom had a right to his opinion, of course, and with age I have become less prickly. He has since helped the Afton Historical Society Press with images and information for several of our book projects for which we are very grateful. For my part, I'd love to publish a fuller account of this Eastman Johnson collection should a qualified author wish to take on this project.

Lake Superior Indians sold well in this country and also abroad. On the advice of a friend whose book was being distributed by the University of Washington Press, we contacted the marketing director there. The University of Washington Press ended up distributing *Lake Superior Indians* both nationally and internationally. (In 1999, during a trip to New York for the Afton Historical Society Press, I visited the Brooklyn Museum to see a traveling exhibition of Eastman Johnson's artwork and was delighted to find *Lake Superior Indians* for sale in the museum shop, sixteen years after it was first published.)

Self-publishing only got easier after that. I began not one but two new books: *Minnesota's Irish* and *Pretty Red Wing: Historic River Town*. Two weeks before St. Patrick's Day in 1984, *Minnesota's Irish* was in virtually every bookstore window in the state. Many stores built entire displays around this single book. *Minnesota's Irish* was the first book to focus on the state's large Irish contingent, and in Minnesota, St. Patrick's Day ranks second only to Christmas in terms of book sales.

Minnesota's Irish grew out of a longtime fascination with my own Irish heritage. My Condon great-grandparents

My great-grandparents,
John and Mary White Condon

emigrated to this country in the wake of the 1840s potato famines. Most of Minnesota's Irish share a similar legacy. In the book I included chapters about the state's earliest Irish settlers; Archbishop John Ireland's Irish colonies in southwestern Minnesota; the archbishop's sister Ellen Ireland (from my earlier profile for *Minnesota History*); F. Scott Fitzgerald (the first major American novelist of Irish descent); oil-rich Ignatius Aloysius O'Shaughnessy (a leading benefactor of the Catholic Church in this country and abroad); and the annual St. Patrick's Day parades in St. Paul (to which Archbishop Ireland once called a halt after the celebrations had turned into what he termed "midnight orgies").

On March 6, I wrote in my diary: "What did I do right! I am really overwhelmed by what is happening with *Minnesota's Irish*. This morning I taped a 'Minnesota Memories' segment with Beth Wood for the *Good Company* show [KSTP-TV] at MacCafferty's Irish Pub in St. Paul. This kind of thing is getting a little easier. I remembered more of the answers. This will air on Tuesday, March 13. We changed the date of the book signing at MacCafferty's to March 15 to take advantage of this publicity. I dropped off a press release for the book at the St. Paul paper. Bookmen ordered another 200 books. Mary Ann Grossmann called and said the paper would like to excerpt from *Minnesota's Irish* on St. Patrick's Day. She offered me $100!"

We were learning more about marketing. To help draw

attention to the book, we sold and gave away *Minnesota's Irish* T-shirts that year—kelly green, they were, with white lettering and shamrocks. I also approached the Grotto Foundation in St. Paul which agreed to help support this book by purchasing four hundred copies for Sisters of St. Joseph convents in several states. Volunteers at the College of St. Catherine did the mailing. The Grotto Foundation was funded by a grandson of James J. Hill. Two generations earlier, the railroad magnate and his wife Mary had been close friends and benefactors of Archbishop John Ireland and his sister, Ellen Ireland. Hill money had built the St. Paul seminary in 1894.

Archbishop John Ireland's funeral procession in 1918 was the largest ever seen in St. Paul.

Later that year, in time for Christmas, we published *Pretty Red Wing: Historic River Town*. Like the earlier Stillwater book, it was an illustrated history of a popular nineteenth-century river town. I did most of my research at the Goodhue County Historical Society, which is less than an hour's drive from Afton. Jean Chesley was president and pointed me in all the right directions. Jean's father, Dr. Alexander Anderson, had discovered and patented the process of puffing cereal grains. (Puffed rice at first was considered a confection and sold like popcorn at the World's Fair in St. Louis in 1904.)

The Goodhue County Historical Society provided historic photographs for the book, which we supplemented with some present-day photos taken by Charlie.

The cover illustration for *Pretty Red Wing* was a brightly colored image of a young Indian woman in a feathered headdress from the vintage sheet music for a Tin Pan Alley tune titled "Red Wing." As a child I had listened time and again to this song on my mother's old Edison cylinder phonograph: "There once lived an Indian maid, A shy little prairie maid . . ." The sheet music had been published in 1907 and was no longer under copyright so to help advertise the book, we re-printed the sheet music and put a full-page ad for the new book on the back cover. We paid for printing the sheet music by selling advertisements on the inside back page to Red Wing businessmen.

On July 12, 1984, I noted in my diary: "Dale finished the dummy for the Red Wing book. I made sales calls in Red Wing yesterday. I stopped first to see Alice Lane at the Red Wing Book Company in the St. James Hotel. She ordered 700 books and 100 pieces of sheet music. I agreed to come to the store on two Saturdays to sign books, one in November and one in December. Manager Gene Foster at the St. James ordered 100 books to put in the hotel's guest rooms. Altogether I sold 867 books, 145 pieces of music, and $135 worth of advertising for a grand total of $7,306.29!

During the weeks that followed, I sold several Red Wing businesses on the idea of purchasing books to use as Christmas gifts for their employees. I also called on Dr. Dan Mjolness, Red Wing's superintendent of schools. I told him that we would like to be able to provide a copy of the book for each classroom and each teacher in his system at Christmastime and that area businessmen to whom I had spoken were willing to help foot the bill. Dr. Mjolness liked the idea and said that the school system could also partial ly fund this project. He calculated that he could use about 450 books. Area businessmen ended up supplying about two-thirds of that number, and Dr. Mjolness gave me a purchase order for the balance.

In early December, a day before my first book signing for *Pretty Red Wing*, at the Red Wing Book Company, the *Red Wing Republican Eagle* carried a front-page article by staff writer Ruth Nerhaugen (with whom I had had lunch on more than one occasion): "*Pretty Red Wing: Historic River Town* has appeared in local bookstores just in time for the Christmas shopping season. . . . There's no question, the volume will find its way under many Christmas trees." With Ruth's help, it did. The signing was one of the busiest I have ever done, with people lined up all afternoon. Charlie and I and bookseller Alice Lane toasted our success before dinner that evening in the very elegant Victorian Dining Room at the St. James Hotel. (What I remember most about that dinner was that the room was so dimly lit that Charlie couldn't read the menu. When he told this to the waiter, the man brought him a penlight. We all thought this was pretty hilarious.)

The key to a successful bookstore signing is publicity and more publicity. Without a lot of drumming up of interest in you and your book, they will fail every time. One time nobody came into the store I was sitting in all afternoon.

What's worse is when there are people in the store but they don't have any interest in you or your book. There you are, alone at a table in the middle of a store, waiting for someone to talk to you. I suspect every author can tell you horror stories. I once heard Jon Hassler speak after finishing a national book tour. He said that he had sat in fifty-some stores and only signed a few more books than that.

Jon is one of my all-time favorite authors and exceptionally modest and unassuming. On another occasion, I was in the audience with a group of librarians when he told a story about Minnesota being the kind of place where you didn't get a swelled head. Jon had found a number of one of his books on a "remainders" table in a Minneapolis bookstore. The price was less than what he could buy the books for from his publisher, and his nieces and nephews might like to have copies, he reasoned, so he picked them all up and took them to the cash register.

"You must like this book," said the girl at the register. "I do," Jon answered, "I wrote it," and he showed her his picture on the book's back cover. Whereupon the girl called for the manager. The manager arrived, Jon thinking all the while that the man would probably want to shake his hand. But no. The girl had called the manager to OK Jon's check.

In late 1985 our fifth and final Johnston Publishing project was *The Minnesota Christmas Book*, a big red book, twelve inches square, and fairly expensive at $27.50. In it I described some of the special ways in which Minnesotans celebrate the holiday, including but not limited to their religious ceremonies, immigrant customs, children's toys and dolls, books, Christmas at the governor's mansion, and the Tyrone Guthrie Theater's annual production of "A Christmas Carol." There were recipes from the historic Alexander Ramsey House kitchen and John Schumacher's

New Prague Hotel. Byerly's (a local grocery chain) provided the menu for an after-the-theater holiday buffet. Charlie produced a splendid portfolio of full-page black-and-white photographs that we reproduced in duotone to illustrate this book.

We had something of a track record by now, and Mary Ann Grossmann called before we even had books. She had heard the Christmas book was coming and asked me to be sure to send her a copy. One of the first copies also went to Barbara Flanagan at the *Minneapolis Star Tribune*. Barbara wrote back saying

Father Christmas at Riverplace in Minneapolis, 1984,
from The Minnesota Christmas Book

she thought this might be our best book so far. *Mpls/St. Paul* magazine editor Brian Anderson paid us $200 for an excerpt for his December issue. Minnesota Governor Rudy Perpich ordered copies to use as Christmas gifts for dignitaries in this country and abroad.

The Minnesota Christmas Book was a fitting finale to our publishing efforts. We had produced five good books in four years and decided to quit while we were ahead. Self-publishing had been a deliciously satisfying experience, and one that I would heartily encourage others to try. Many, many good books might never be published except for writers who take it upon themselves to see their work through to print.

Self-publishing entails commitment and a great deal of

work, but the payback can be terrific, beginning with the exhil-
aration you will feel when the printer hands you the first
bound copy of your very own book. It can also be financially
rewarding, although Johnston Publishing books actually never
made much money. We weren't in it for the money. We had simply wanted to produce quality books, and I was always more
interested in writing them than selling them.

Eventually, I wound up feeling drained and fragmented
from wearing so many hats, which on any given day could
include writer, editor, publicist, salesperson, and shipping
clerk. I wanted to forget about marketing and concentrate on
writing. I always had several magazine articles underway, and
I had begun writing art-related articles on a regular basis for
Sporting Classics magazine in Camden, South Carolina, and
Wildlife Art News in Minneapolis. My first piece for *Sporting
Classics*, about wildlife artist Francis Lee Jaques, would lead in
1994 to my first book for the Afton Historical Society Press: *The
Shape of Things: The Art of Francis Lee Jaques.*

But there were more books to come before that, and I also
felt it was finally time to upgrade my limited education.

6

College Made Easy

IN 1986 I WENT to college. I didn't actually *go* to school in the usual sense, but I did earn a Bachelor of Arts degree. Fair and square. Thanks to a wonderful program at Metropolitan State University, I was able to obtain a college degree without attending classes.

As I think back and try to sort out the reasons I felt I needed a college diploma, I can identify several. First of all, even though I was functioning successfully as a free-lance writer, I still felt like something of an imposter without one. I hated having to admit on occasion that I only had a high-school education. I was also thinking long and hard about what I might like to do in the future. Charlie had suffered a heart attack during our self-publishing flurry. Perhaps I would one day need to have a regular job with benefits. Perhaps I would one day *like* to have an exciting job with benefits. I daydreamed about working for the Minnesota Historical Society or the Minneapolis Institute of Arts in some challenging capacity.

After much soul-searching (I used to ponder how to best use the rest of my life during Mass on Sundays), I convinced myself that I was probably meant to teach American history or American art history at the college level. Why hadn't I seen it? This was what so much of my research and writing had been leading up to! To do so, however, I would no doubt need a Ph.D., and I didn't have so much as a single college credit. Over the years I had been eligible to attend classes free of charge at the College of St. Thomas in St. Paul when we had children there, but this opportunity had never appealed to me. I hadn't wanted to spend time in a classroom.

I still didn't want to take time out from writing to attend classes, but as it turned out, at least for my undergraduate degree, I didn't have to. When I mentioned one day to editor John Hodowanic at *Twin Cities* magazine that I was thinking about going back to school, he suggested that I get in touch with President Reatha King at Metropolitan State University in St. Paul. Metropolitan was affiliated with the University of Minnesota and offered, in addition to classes, several non-traditional methods for earning college credits.

I was forty-six at the time and in a hurry to get on with my education, to move into my intended career as a teacher. Could I hope to earn a Ph.D. by the time I was fifty? I asked Dr. King. She thought that I probably could. The first step was to complete my undergraduate degree at Metropolitan, and I could begin earning credits by taking "College-level Examination Program" (CLEP) tests.

This was the easiest and cheapest way to obtain credits. Metropolitan allowed students to test out of a maximum of two years of college courses and offered the tests one Saturday morning each month. The tests cost thirty dollars apiece, so for a few hundred dollars you could be well on your way to a degree. Students could sign up for a maximum of four tests a month, so I took one test each hour from eight in the morning until noon on the designated Saturday.

In six months' time, beginning in January, I tested out of two years of college. I actually loved these exams. I couldn't wait for the given Saturday each month to take them. Just picking out the offerings from the catalog of exams was fun. I chose English Literature, English Composition, American Literature, Analysis and Interpretation of Literature, Sociology, Psychology, American Government, Humanities, American History I and II, and Western Civilization I and II, twenty-four classes in all. The tests were all multiple choice, and maybe I got lucky. I had expected to do fairly well in the English and history subjects, but I even scored a 96 in Sociology. Psychology and Sociology were out of my realm, so I read college texts that our children had at home before taking these two tests.

I was now eligible to become a degree candidate! I was assigned to advisor Carol Ryan (I know this from one slim folder that contains all the information I have concerning my college career, but I don't remember Ms. Ryan). A degree candidate wrote his or her own degree plan and also an "Educational Goals Statement," which I did, probably with her help. For one part of the Educational Goals Statement, students read a number of essays by leading educators on the importance of a liberal arts education and what it meant to be an educated person. We were then asked to summarize these thoughts in our own words. Two paragraphs from my Educational Goals Statement provided new inspiration for me when I read them again recently:

> My idea of an educated person (and I'm speaking of a liberally educated person) is one who recognizes, first of all, that learning is a lifelong pursuit, and secondly, that learning not only heightens the pleasure of living, but adds purpose and direction to one's existence. The lessons of history make it clear that only by exposing ourselves to the humanities, including philosophy, history, literature, art, and music, can we transcend the ordinary and venal, to stretch our imaginations, and to be all that we can be.

One's education, of course, can be carried on in virtually any arena; certainly, all learning doesn't take place in the classroom. Importantly, an educated person has learned to think clearly and logically, make critical analyses and decisions, and expresses himself or herself verbally, or on the written page, with a certain amount of grace. As the circle completes itself, not surprisingly, an educated person learns to know and accept one's self, a condition that brings with it the peace of mind that nurtures continual growth.

My degree plan addressed the five competence areas identified and required by Metropolitan that led to a well-rounded, liberal, education: "Communication"; "Vocation"; "Community"; "Culture, Science, and Tradition"; and "Avocation." You had to have a certain number of credits in each of these categories in order to graduate. My CLEP credits already partially addressed these requirements. I listed English credits under "Communication"; History courses under "Vocation"; Sociology and Psychology under "Community"; Humanities under "Culture, Science, and Tradition"; and English and American Literature under "Avocation."

Once I had completed all the CLEP tests allowed, I was able to earn my last two years' credits entirely through so-called "prior learning assessments." This proved easier and more fun than the CLEP tests. For a "prior," you simply had to prove your competence in an upper division course that you had selected from virtually any college catalog. The evaluator was either a qualified Metropolitan staff member or an outside expert with appropriate credentials. The student could suggest outside evaluators. I asked anthropologist Dr. Lou Casagrande to review my "prior competence" in courses titled "Plains Indians Cultures" and "Southwest Indian Studies," for instance. Lou was one of Charlie's colleagues at the Science Museum of Minnesota.

During the summer, after preparing my degree plan, I

went ahead and wrote up twenty-two prior competencies that I wanted to have evaluated: Writing Magazine Articles, Writing Major Projects, Book Publishing, Painting in Minnesota, Eastman Johnson in Minnesota, American Painters, American Western Art, American Illustration, Museum Conservation, Music in Minnesota, Irish Studies, The Irish in America, The History of St. Paul, The History of the St. Croix Valley, The History of the Hiawatha Valley, The Historian as Investigator, Interviewing, Public Speaking, Publicity, Marketing, Professional Selling, and Piano.

Except for Piano (which I had taught both at home and at St. Mark's Convent when we lived in St. Paul), all of my competencies relied on experience I had gained by writing magazine articles and self-publishing my five books. There was a one-page form for each prior that asked for a description of the competency and the manner in which it was achieved. For "The Irish in America," I wrote:

> Knows history and can interpret the role of the Irish in America, with particular reference to Irish immigrants and their descendants in Minnesota, well enough to write magazine articles and book.

To prove my competence, I submitted a copy of my book *Minnesota's Irish* (1984) and two magazine articles: "Reflected Glory: The Story of Ellen Ireland" (*Minnesota History*, 1982) and "Great Gatsby! Scott and Zelda Are Coming Home" (*Twin Cities*, 1982).

For "Book Publishing," I wrote: "Knows principles and methods of publishing, particularly self-publishing, including determining audience, writing and editing manuscripts, and arranging production and distribution, and can publish general trade books. I submitted copies of all five Johnston Publishing books.

For "Publicity," I stated: "Knows principles and methods of obtaining local and national publicity at a professional level." I had a whole portfolio of press clippings for my various books and notes on radio and television interviews.

Once they were approved, the priors would complete my degree work, but I was getting ahead of myself. I could not even register for these priors until my degree plan itself had been approved, and this hadn't happened. On September 15 I wrote to Reatha King:

> I'm back asking for your help again. The problem is that with Carol Ryan gone, I am currently without an advisor. . . .
>
> Some months ago, Carol suggested that I stop and see her advisor in the history department at the University [of Minnesota], Professor Clarke Chambers, and go over my proposed degree plan at Metro with him. As it turned out, Professor Chambers said that I could register for graduate classes this fall if I wanted to (which I did), and I know that he pulled a few strings to arrange this. I will receive graduate credit for these classes, but only after I have a B.A. from Metro. Also, to formally apply to the graduate school for winter quarter, I need to have my B.A. by their application deadline, November 25.
>
> I am waiting now for my degree plan to be approved. Until it is, I cannot register for prior competencies. I've written twenty-two prior competencies, and I'd like to begin having them evaluated immediately. Is this possible? Is it possible to meet the November 25 deadline for a B.A.?"

It was and I did. Metropolitan's letter congratulating me upon being accepted as a degree candidate arrived in a few days. The prior learning assessments were more expensive than the CLEP tests but still a bargain at $114.25 apiece. I appeared at Metropolitan's registrar's office with a check for $2,513.50 to register for all twenty-two competencies. The woman to whom I tried to give my money said she did not think she could take it; no one had ever registered for that many competencies at one time. Dr. King's office intervened and sent word that it was OK to accept my money and applications.

All of my prior competencies passed muster. Professor Clarke Chambers evaluated my proficiency in "The Irish in America":

> These pieces [referring to my book and articles] demonstrate a fine grasp of Irish-American history and of the methods of historical research and writing. Clearly Ms. Johnston is familiar with secondary works, and the large cultural context within which her studies fall. She has used primary records critically and wisely, including oral interviews. She writes with clarity and grace, and with the precision and accuracy that are the mark of a sophisticated historian.
>
> The level of quality is as high as one expects from an established professional scholar.

Dr. Lou Casagrande (who had recently written a glowing one-page review of my book *Lake Superior Indians* for the Science Museum's *Encounters* magazine) assessed my prior competence in "Plains Indian Cultures":

> Pat Johnston has clearly acquired the research and archival skills necessary to interpret the cultures of the American Indian for an enlightened general public. In particular, her articles reveal a consistent and perceptive understanding of how earlier artists, photographers, etc., portrayed the Indian and how these earlier images reflected a broader historical context. Pat's work *significantly* exceeds what I would consider an adequate undergraduate level of competence in the interpretation of Indian culture.

I was liking school better all the time! Legendary St. Paul newspaper man Gareth Hiebert judged my competence in "The History of the Hiawatha Valley" (wherein lies pretty Red Wing): "As one of Minnesota's top authors in the late 20th century, Pat certainly has fulfilled the objectives and goals of this project." Metropolitan faculty member David Farkell reviewed my expertise in "Publicity": "Ms. Johnston has a knack for placing publicity at appropriate times in appropriate media and getting results. There is no question that she has achieved the competence." I can see why I saved these papers!

While my competencies were being evaluated that fall, I was already taking two graduate-level classes in the History Department at the University of Minnesota. Clarke Chambers had agreed to act as my advisor and arranged for me to enroll as an "Adult Special." This meant that I would receive graduate credit for these classes once I was accepted as a graduate student. I was studying historiography ("Scope and Methods of Historical Studies") with Professor George Green and "The Celtic World" with Professor Fred Suppe.

George Green introduced his class to numerous books by historians about how to write history and also recognize our particular biases when doing so. I remember really liking George and that we presented our final papers at a potluck supper at his roomy, older home in the St. Anthony Park area of Minneapolis. I took my favorite wild rice and chicken casserole. I don't recall anything about my paper, only that George gave me an "A" for it and his course. I had a harder time earning an "A" from Fred Suppe for "The Celtic World" and had to rewrite a paper to do so, but I came away from his class with an increased appreciation of my Celtic heritage.

By November 25, I had my baccalaureate degree, and I was admitted to the University as a graduate student in the History Department beginning winter quarter. My plan was to attend school full-time beginning in January to make quick work of my master's degree. In December, however, I was contacted by editor Mark Thompson at American

Geographic Publishing in Helena, Montana, who asked me to write the text for an illustrated book titled *Minnesota: Portrait of the Land and Its People*.

This was a very tempting proposition. The subject matter was just right for me, and I weighed the merits of doing the book versus attending classes. On the plus side, writing the book would be more fun, and the oncoming winter was another consideration. It can sometimes be very difficult to get around in Minnesota in winter. I considered the possibility of not being able to get to some classes at the University or being stuck there in a snowstorm. The more I thought about it, the more it seemed like a good idea to stay home and write that winter.

As it turned out, I was able to continue earning graduate credits while doing so. Clarke Chambers suggested that I work with U of M Regents' Professor of Geography John Borchert on this book. Professor Borchert allowed me to register for three independent study credits in geography for writing it, and he agreed to critique it. His input also made for a better book, of course.

I had a great deal of enthusiasm for this book project. "To my mind, there is no finer place to live than in Minnesota," I wrote in the short Preface. "The center of my personal universe, it is moreover a national center for industry, education, medicine, and the arts. There are four times as many millionaires per capita in Minnesota as in Texas.

There are more theater goers per capita in the Twin Cities than in New York City. And the Minneapolis/St. Paul campus of the University of Minnesota has the largest enrollment of any single campus in the United States." WOW! It's good to be reminded occasionally what we really have here.

Writing a book-length manuscript is really not much different than writing a magazine piece. It's just longer and takes more time. I tend to think of writing the individual chapters in much the same way that I would think about writing a lengthy magazine article. *Minnesota: Portrait of the Land and Its People*, for instance, is comprised of nine chapters, each of them about five thousand words—about the same length as the profiles of Minnesotans I wrote for *Minnesota History*. Each chapter, like each article, needs an interesting beginning, a meaty mid-section, and a good ending.

I divided this book into the following chapters:

1. SHAPED BY STREAMS
2. THE LAND: PreCambrian Time to the Present
3. THE PEOPLES: Indians to Immigrants
4. THE TWIN CITIES: Models for Urban America
5. SOUTHEASTERN TRIANGLE: A River-Town Medley
6. SOUTHWESTERN MINNESOTA: Speaking of Farming
7. MINNESOTA'S HEARTLAND: Maker of Myth
8. ARROWHEAD REGION: Siren of the North
9. NORTHWESTERN MINNESOTA: Ice-Age Inheritance

Right on deadline, I completed the manuscript by June 30. American Geographic had asked for and received approximately forty thousand words, for which I was paid $7,000. The editors did most of the work of securing excellent color photos for the book. They also used several of Charlie's, and even one that I had taken of the Depot

Museum in Duluth. We were paid additionally for these, depending upon the size the photo appeared in the book. *Minnesota: Portrait of the Land and Its People* is still a good-looking book and one that I'm proud to have written. The last I heard, it was being distributed for American Geographic by Random House in New York.

By the time I had completed the Minnesota book, I had also signed contracts for two additional book projects. First, I had won a contract to write a centennial history of the White Bear Yacht Club. I felt good about getting this commission. The yacht club committee had interviewed several prospective writers, among them former Minnesota Historical Society Director Russell Fridley who flew in from out of town. Fridley, I'm guessing, probably asked for more money than I did.

Within weeks of the yacht club interview, I also received a commission that would change my life. I was asked to meet with Cargill heir and director W. Duncan MacMillan at Cargill headquarters in Wayzata, Minnesota, just west of Minneapolis. Mr. MacMillan asked me if I would be willing to work with him on a family history that he wanted to publish privately for his family. This offer was too good to turn down, and I didn't.

The White Bear Yacht Club, 1988

I began working with Duncan MacMillan in July 1987. I still had my sights set on a Ph.D., however, and managed to fit in a graduate-level workshop about Indians in Minnesota at the Minnesota Historical Society that month. This was a two-week, all-day, introduction to teaching state and local history. I looked at this class as something of a vacation. We took field trips to the James J. Hill House on Summit Avenue and to Fort Snelling. We also had some very good speakers including several Native Americans. Our final grade was based on an essay on a preapproved topic. I titled my paper "Charles Alexander Eastman (Ohiyesa): Acculturated Indian."

Charles Alexander Eastman (Ohiyesa)

Dr. Charles Eastman had long fascinated me and I had even considered writing a book about him, except that scholar Raymond Wilson beat me to it (*Ohiyesa: Charles Eastman, Santee Sioux*, University of Illinois Press, 1983). A physician and author, Charles Eastman was the best-educated and best-known Indian in this country by the first decade of the twentieth century. In 1905 he was among the dignitaries invited to Mark Twain's seventieth birthday party at Delmonico's in New York (where he was pictured in formal attire at a table of dignitaries). Influential Indian rights reformers considered him the foremost example of what an Indian could achieve, and Eastman seemed living proof that assimilation was the answer to this nation's Indian problem.

Or was he? What reformers usually failed to recognize was that Eastman was an acculturated rather than an assimilated Indian.

I had first stumbled onto this larger-than-life Dakota (Sioux) Indian while doing research on his white grandfather, soldier painter Seth Eastman, for an article for *American History Illustrated*. While posted to Fort Snelling in what later became Minnesota, Second Lieutenant Seth Eastman had married the daughter of Chief Cloudman of the Lake Calhoun village, a girl named Wakaninajinwin (Stands Like a Spirit). In 1831 Stands Like a Spirit gave birth to their daughter, Mary Nancy Eastman. Shortly afterwards, Eastman was reassigned to topographical duty in Louisiana. Stands Like a Spirit and her daughter stayed behind with her people.

Nancy Eastman, as she was known, grew to beautiful young womanhood in the shadow of Fort Snelling, married young, when she was sixteen, and bore her Indian husband five children. She died in her twenties following the birth of the youngest child in 1858, a boy who was called Hakadah (The Pitiful Last). At the age of four, for a feat of bravery, Hakadah was awarded the proud name of Ohiyesa (The Winner). Following the Sioux Uprising in 1862 (now known as the Dakota War), little Ohiyesa was carried by fleeing Indians to Canada, where he was trained by an uncle to be a skillful hunter and warrior. He grew up believing that his father, Many Lightnings, was one of the thirty-eight "hostiles" hanged in a mass execution at Mankato, Minnesota.

But his father hadn't been hanged. Instead, Many Lightnings was among the more than two hundred Indians whose death sentences were commuted to three years' imprisonment by President Lincoln. While he was incarcerated at the federal penitentiary at Davenport, Iowa, Many Lightnings converted to Christianity and adopted the name of Jacob

*Charles Eastman in 1890 at
Boston School of Medicine*

and his dead wife's surname, Eastman. He later took up residence in the Sioux community of Flandreau, South Dakota, and began searching for his lost son. After ten years' separation, Jacob found Ohiyesa camped with members of his tribe in Manitoba. The youth, now fifteen, who had just returned from a hunt, agreed to go with his father back to Flandreau.

Ohiyesa would never feel wholly at ease in the white man's world, but he acquiesced to his father's wishes and learned to read and write English at the mission school at Flandreau. He converted to Christianity, taking the name Charles Alexander Eastman, and continued his education at the Santee Normal School in Nebraska and Beloit College in Wisconsin. Wanting to be of service to his people, he decided on a career in medicine, and he went on to graduate from Dartmouth and the Boston University School of Medicine.

Dr. Charles Eastman was the first government physician assigned to Pine Ridge reservation in South Dakota, where he witnessed the Ghost Dance movement and its suppression by federal officials. Following the massacre called Wounded Knee, he helped bring back the dead and cared for the Indian wounded in the Episcopal mission chapel. "We tore out the pews and covered the floor with hay and quilts. There we laid the poor creatures side by side in rows," he wrote sadly.

Shortly after arriving at Pine Ridge, Eastman met Elaine Goodale, the white supervisor of Indian schools in the Dakotas and Nebraska, and the couple was married in

New York City in 1891. Two years later, they moved to St. Paul where Eastman began writing *Indian Boyhood*, the first of several books dealing with his Indian heritage. He also became a missionary for the YMCA, organizing forty-three Indian groups in the United States and Canada. At the behest of tribal leaders he went to Washington to lobby for treaty monies due the Dakota. Under President Theodore Roosevelt, he helped revise tribal allotment roles, convinced that he was working in the best interests of his people.

Elaine Goodale Eastman

His life was not particularly happy. He and Elaine raised six children, five daughters and a son, in white communities, but later lived apart. His medical practice did not flourish, perhaps because white patients preferred white physicians, and he devoted more and more of his time to writing and lecturing. He belonged to two worlds and had managed to adjust to an alien culture but eventually became disillusioned with the Christian civilization, which did not practice what it preached. Elaine Eastman preached assimilation for all Indians, but her marriage to Charles was an experiment that went awry. In old age,

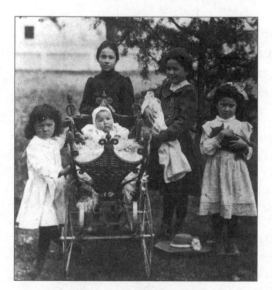

Five of the six Eastman children, left to right, Ohiyesa II, baby Eleanor, Dora, Irene, and Virginia

Charles Eastman retreated to an island to live life on his own terms, by himself.

I had collected all of Charles Eastman's ten books and gone to great lengths to learn all I could about him long before taking the workshop at the Minnesota Historical Society. Charlie and I had traveled to South Dakota to review the papers of a nun who had received a grant from the National Endowment for the Humanities to write a biography about Eastman and then died without completing it. Another time, when we were in Washington, D. C., to interview Joan Mondale for a *Collector Editions* article, I had spent time in the National Archives reading Eastman's correspondence from Pine Ridge with government officials. I had actually held his handwritten letters in *my* hands.

I was glad to be able to use some of this material for my Minnesota Historical Society class essay and enjoyed writing it, confident that it was a good paper. I typed up a flawless copy and delivered it on the last day of the workshop to instructor Thomas Thompson. Thompson, however, didn't think it was all that great. After reading it, he returned my paper by mail with this unenthusiastic note:

> This is an informative, well-written essay about Eastman. However, it does not include the detailed look at primary sources that is necessary for this class. Your sources are interesting, but not used thoroughly as the springboard for your essay.
>
> Course grade: B
> —Tom

The "B" gave me quite a jolt. Less than a year before, I had been "one of Minnesota's top authors in the late 20th century," who wrote "with the precision and accuracy that are the mark of a sophisticated historian." Now I had just spent two weeks and more than five hundred dollars for a "B"! In that same time I could have produced a magazine article for which I would have been *paid* five hundred dollars. That "B" marked another turning point in my life.

I wasn't ready yet to give up my dream of a Ph.D., but I did send Clarke Chambers a note in early September explaining that I had decided to abandon the idea of taking a class with him that fall. "What with three book projects to complete, I seem to have all the work I can handle," I wrote. (Besides the White Bear Yacht Club book and the MacMillan project, I was also editing a centennial history of St. Luke's Catholic Church in St. Paul.) "Just now, I'm packing up to spend a couple of weeks researching the MacMillan family history in the Montreal-Quebec area. Charlie's going along, so we're making a holiday of this as well."

Clarke (who always wrote warm and witty letters) replied:

> My response to your recent letter is ambivalent—not distant or neutral—but torn!
>
> On the one side, I had looked forward to your being in the seminar because I know you would bring to the group different perspectives and talents. On the other hand, clearly your commitments make it impossible to shoehorn in a demanding seminar.
>
> At the rate your projects are accumulating—and there's a book or monographic piece at the end of every one—the certification part of your graduate study recedes in significance.
>
> You will find me an open and accepting 'father'—when you darken my door again, you will be enthusiastically welcomed.

That is the last letter in my "college" file. I never officially quit college, but I never found time to go back. For the next couple of years, the yacht club and MacMillan projects were all consuming (along with the occasional magazine piece that was too interesting to pass up). The idea of one day teaching in a college or university began diminishing in appeal as it became more and more apparent to me that per-haps I was already doing what I was really best at—writing. I was also making good money doing it.

If I stopped to think about it, I already had the college degree I'd always wanted. Maybe I didn't need an advanced degree. Maybe I wasn't cut out for a career in teaching after all. Maybe I wasn't even interested in a career in teaching any-more. The older I get, the more uncomfortable I know I would be in a classroom. I am very comfortable as a writer. I like working alone, at my own pace, in a room of my own. So was obtaining a college degree wasted on me? Not at all. For about four thousand dollars, I gained immeasurable self-esteem. I learned that, on my own, through my writing, I had actually achieved at least the equivalent of a college education.

Charlie reminded me recently about the cowardly lion in *The Wizard of Oz* who wanted the wizard to give him courage. The wizard told the lion he was already coura-geous and brave, that maybe all he needed was a medal to prove it. In my case, Metropolitan gave me the medal I needed to prove I was educated, a bronze medallion about one and one-half inches in diameter. On one side it says "Metropolitan State University"; on the other, "Bachelor of Arts." It came on a brown cord to hang around my neck and arrived in the mail along with my Bachelor of Arts diploma.

7

MacGhillemhaoil

I BEGAN WORKING WITH CARGILL director and heir
W. Duncan MacMillan in July 1987. One day, out of the blue,
I received a call from his office, asking me if I would be
interested in helping him write and produce a book about
the history of his family. You bet I would! I knew enough
about the MacMillans to know that they are one of the most
prominent families in the world. The MacMillans and their
Cargill cousins are today
the owners of the largest
privately held company on
the face of the earth:
Cargill, Inc.

Over the next several
years, I would spend hun-
dreds of hours talking with
Duncan and composing and
reviewing manuscript chapters with him, sometimes at
his home, but more often in

Cargill world headquarters in Wayzata

his office at the Cargill Office Center—a three-story office complex that adjoins Cargill's world headquarters in the former
Rufus Rand mansion on Lake Minnetonka. In 1946, bucking

conventional business wisdom by leaving the thriving Minneapolis commercial district, Duncan's father, Cargill President John H. MacMillan, Jr., had moved Cargill's executive offices from the downtown Grain Exchange to this sprawling, steep-roofed house on more than two hundred acres overlooking Gray's Bay, fifteen minutes west of Minneapolis.

Duncan and I eventually produced not one book but two—a glorious, two-volume work in beautiful color titled *MacGhillemhaoil* (Mock'-gheelia-vul—MacMillan in Gaelic). Designed by Dale Johnston, my former partner in Johnston Publishing, and printed in Minneapolis, these books were handbound in MacMillan tartans by Gregor Campbell at his Campbell-Logan Bindery in Minneapolis. Limited to five hundred privately-printed copies, for Duncan's family and friends, *MacGhillemhaoil* would be the basis for a trade edition of the MacMillan story: *MacMillan: The American Grain Family*, published by the Afton Historical Society Press in 1998.

Each of my writing projects has been a stepping stone to my present position as publisher at the Afton Press, and my work with Duncan was one *gigantic* step. Our work together on his family history led directly to the formation of the Afton Historical Society Press. But I'm getting ahead of myself.

On that first summer afternoon in 1987 when we met in his office—a large, sunny, corner room with dozens of duck stamp and other wildlife art prints on the walls—Duncan told me that he had been a classics major at Brown University. He was intensely interested in the past, he said, and for the last twenty years had been delving into his family history in libraries in this country and abroad. He had amassed file cabinets filled with family papers and photographs, and he had also recently hired research help to fill in some of the gaps. He wanted to leave the best record of his family that he could for future generations.

The MacMillans, I was about to learn, trace their ances-try to MacBeth, who was neither the bloodthirsty villain nor despicable usurper that Shakespeare made him out to be. The historic MacBeth had a three-fold claim to the Scottish throne. He was a holy man, beloved by his Highland fol-lowers, and Scotland prospered during his sixteen-year reign.

One of the oldest Highland clans, the MacMillans are descended from a twelfth-century monk named Gilchrist An Gille Maolan. MacMillan means "son of the little ton-sured one." The first time the name appears in Latin it is inscribed *mac Molini* in the Book of Deer, a record of land grants and offerings made to the Celtic Church between 1000 and 1150 A.D. During the next several centuries it is found in various English documents as *MacMolan* in 1263, *Macmolane* in 1452, *McMulane* in 1505, *McMillane* in 1632, and *Mcmillen* in 1641. By 1745, when Bonnie Prince Charlie landed in Scotland to lead his Jacobite clansmen in a last desperate attempt to regain the British throne for the Stuarts, the name was being spelled *McKmillan*, *McMilland*, *McMullan*, *MacMylan*, and *MacMyllan*.

Clinging to a long-established family pattern, Duncan's great-grandfather and his father and grandfather before him went by "McMillan." Sometime in the early 1890s, when he was twenty-three or twenty-four years old, his grandfather, John H. MacMillan, Sr., born and bred in the American Midwest, adopted the spelling used today by Duncan's branch of the family. Whatever his personal reasons for doing so—some family members have suggested that "Mc," meaning "son of," was the abbreviated English version of the more authentic Scottish "Mac"—he also marked the beginning of a new era for his branch of the family.

As a *MacMillan*, John H., Sr. parented the present-day

John H. MacMillan, Sr.

grain family. Credited with salvaging the foundering Cargill Elevator Company in the early 1900s, he delivered it from the jaws of its creditors and set the family on the course that continues to provide its (very ample) livelihood.

The first of Duncan's progenitors to come to North America was a foot soldier, John McMillan of Glen Nevis, who fought with the English hero James Wolfe at the Battle of Quebec in 1759. After six years service with the 78th Highland Frasers, and having helped win the New World stage on which his descendants would play out their destinies, John McMillan returned home to Glen Nevis where he married and raised a large family.

In 1815 John's son, Duncan Ban McMillan, would be the first person to apply for passage to North America aboard a government-sponsored emigrant vessel. To help resolve Scotland's growing overpopulation problem and also to further British aims on this continent, His Majesty's government was offering prospective settlers free transportation to Quebec, one hundred acres of land, free rations for six months, and farm implements at cost. The same day's Montreal *Herald* that announced the arrival at Quebec of Duncan Ban's ship, the *Atlas*, carried news of the Duke of Wellington's victory at Waterloo.

In June 1988, Charlie and I flew to Scotland, where several generations of John McMillan's family had been tenant farmers at Achintee Farm in Glen Nevis. I wanted to learn about the everyday lives of the McMillans in Scotland. "It is especially interesting to see how the people's way of life was largely shaped by Highland topography and weather," I reported back to Duncan. "Historians have also had much to say about their rich, intellectual life, dating from when the Highland chiefs held sway, which accounts for their good manners, creativity, and pioneering qualities."

Glen Nevis is a gorgeous place—a narrow, winding glacial valley, rimmed by hunkering mountains. Ten miles long, it ascends four hundred feet above sea level to culminate in a breathtaking rocky gorge and rushing waterfall. The farm where Duncan Ban was born is on the bank of the River Nevis, a fine, clear trout and salmon stream. The McMillans were subsistence farmers who most likely grew potatoes (the mainstay of the Highland diet) along with some grain. They would have had a few black cattle, some goats, and several

The River Nevis in Glen Nevis

small Highland work horses for plowing, harrowing, carrying home peats (for fuel), and hauling manure to the fields.

Today the two-story main house at Achintee Farm caters to bed-and-breakfast guests. Behind it, crouching prettily at the foot of lofty Ben Nevis, Britain's highest hill at 4,406 feet, is the tiny white-washed stone cottage that housed Duncan's McMillan forebears. The sole remaining example of several such tenants' dwellings once clustered at Achintee, the MacMillans' ancestral home is now a self-catering cottage, updated and electrified to accommodate a growing influx of tourists. As many as 1,500 hikers each day converge on this farm to begin their trek up Ben Nevis.

The McMillan cottage in Glen Nevis

"If this project is supposed to be fun, I'm enjoying it immensely," I wrote to Duncan. Our daughter Patty had gone with Charlie and me to Scotland. The minute she heard we were going, she said she was too. She was living in Salt Lake City at the time, but she was able to take the same plane from there that we boarded a few hours later in the Twin Cities for our flight overseas. We stayed in B & Bs our whole time in Scotland, about two weeks, and we learned after a few nights that it didn't matter if there was one, two, or three of us in a room, that we were charged per person, usually about seven or eight British pounds apiece.

I had started out by asking for accommodations for three people, and I was always shown one room with a double bed and a cot for Patty, until I learned that we could have *two* rooms and all of us be more comfortable for the same price. Once when I called ahead and asked for rooms for myself and my husband and daughter, we arrived to find that the room reserved for Patty was a small child's room, with a small, wee bed that tilted from top to bottom. It was quite late by the time we arrived, and the homeowners were surprised to find that Patty was a full grown woman—as surprised as Patty was to find where she would be sleeping that night.

One evening on the Isle of Skye, Patty and I knocked on the door of a B & B that looked like a place that might do for the night. A very old woman answered the door and showed us two rooms. I was about to tell her we would take them when Patty told the woman we were sorry, but we wouldn't be staying. Outside she said to me, "Mom, didn't you notice that she was hard of hearing and that the television she was watching was blaring, right next to the bedrooms?"

It was *so* nice having Patty with us, driving through Scotland with her riding in the back seat. We'd picnic on bread and cheese in cemeteries at lunchtime and eat supper in picturesque roadside inns. She kept us laughing a lot of the time with her wonderful sense of humor and helped me take notes at all the appropriate places, while Charlie was busy making sketches or taking photographs. Along with getting done what we had come for, we were also able to do all the tourist things like visiting castles and walking and shopping the Royal Mile in Edinburgh, so that we all three came home with wonderful memories of this special time together.

As I write this in my upstairs room in Afton, Charlie is downstairs in the kitchen playing old Kenneth McKellar records, 78s, reminding me that we also took the ferry to Oban one evening to hear this glorious Scottish tenor in concert at Corran Hall. This was simply a large wooden-floored hall where we sat on folding chairs facing the stage, but the music was divine, songs like "Roaming in the Gloaming," "The Road to the Isles," "Afton Water," "Westering Home"— the same songs Charlie's playing in the kitchen, making me want to dance for a few minutes, which I'm going to get up and do!

Charlie and I also spent time in Canada. Following our trip to Scotland, we drove up there from Minnesota to inspect the former Duncan Ban McMillan farmstead in Ontario. This hard-working Scotsman cleared a 100-acre Crown grant in Finch Township in Upper Canada (now Ontario). Most of the people in this pioneer farming settlement were emigrants named McMillan who had lost out to sheep in their native Highlands. Soon after arriving in Finch, Duncan Ban married Mary McMillan, who was probably related to him. This intermingling of kin may account for the rare blood disease inherited by the present-day Duncan and his four daughters, all of whom have had their spleens removed to combat chronic hemolytic anemia.

Duncan Ban and Mary McMillan raised ten children in a log house that he eventually replaced with a story-and-a-half residence built from hand-hewn rock quarried on his property. The 1861 census for Finch valued the McMillan property including the new house at $4,200. Forty out of 100 acres were under cultivation. Duncan Ban's harvest that year yielded 150 bushels of oats, 72 bushels of spring wheat, 20 bushels of buckwheat, 100 bushels of potatoes, 44 bushels of peas, and 6 tons of hay. The family also produced 150 pounds of butter, 100 pounds of cheese, 400 pounds of beef, 600 pounds of pork (both the beef and pork were put up in 200-pound barrels), 250 pounds of maple sugar, 27 pounds of wool, and 19 yards of cloth (Duncan Ban had been a weaver in Glasgow). The livestock, valued at $272, included three horses, three sheep, four pigs, four milk cows, and three "steers or heifers under 3 years of age."

Duncan Ban had dabbled in trade in Glasgow, where his mother's relatives were whiskey merchants, but four of his six sons were the first real entrepreneurs in the family.

Emigrating from Canada one and two at a time in the 1850s to Wisconsin, John, Alexander, Ewen Hugh, and Duncan D. McMillan piled up family fortunes as canny loggers in the Black River pineries above La Crosse, and reinvested their profits in real estate and various local businesses.

According to the newspapers at the time, the McMillan brothers cut pretty fancy figures in La Crosse. Alexander,

Duncan D. McMillan

who owned the local gas company and raised blooded horses, drove "the very prettiest, finest and best made cutter we have seen"; Ewen Hugh, who became a lawyer and handled the brothers' business dealings, carried "the best filled tin tobacco box of any man in town"; Duncan D. (Duncan's great-grandfather) wore "a gold watch chain that cost sixty-four dollars and a gold watch that opens with a spring." Duncan D. married Mary Jane McCrea and built the finest house in La Crosse—a princely, red brick Victorian mansion with arched windows and a four-story tower.

In early spring, 1875, the *La Crosse Republican and Leader* carried two seemingly unrelated articles side by side on its front page. The first column reported that Duncan D. and his brother Alexander McMillan, both influential loggers, had purchased a half interest in a water-powered flour mill at nearby West Salem. In a small way, the McMillans were now in the grain business. The second article announced the arrival in town of W. W. Cargill and his pioneer Cargill

William Wallace Cargill

Company. Their two names thus thrown together inadvertently by a newspaper composer, the McMillans and the Cargills would find their lives forevermore entwined.

W. W. (William Wallace) Cargill was born in New York on Long Island in 1844. He was the son of a stout-hearted sea captain from Scotland's Orkney Islands but grew up on a wheat farm in Wisconsin. His mother had insisted on the move inland to prevent her boys from growing up to go to sea. Young Will, after returning home to the farm from civilian duty during the Civil War, set out for Conover, Iowa, a boomtown on the advancing frontier, where he took a job stacking grain in a flathouse along the railroad tracks. In a short time, laying the foundations for an empire, he was operating grain buying stations of his own at Cresco and Lime Springs, Iowa, and Austin, Minnesota. When he moved his company headquarters and his family to La Crosse, the hub of a rail and water transportation network, W. W. Cargill was well on his way to his first million dollars.

Buying property directly across the street from the Duncan D. McMillans, W. W. Cargill erected a flamboyant Victorian brick house run rampant with gables, dormers, and iron roof cresting. The families became best friends, and on a wintry Wednesday evening, February 6, 1895, Will Cargill's eldest daughter, Edna, married her neighbor across the street, Duncan D.'s son, John H. MacMillan. (John H. had recently begun using "Mac" instead of "Mc" when spelling his name.) It was the wedding of the decade in La Crosse and would have far-reaching consequences for both families—not to mention the world grain trade.

Both the McMillan and Cargill families suffered calamitous financial reverses in the years surrounding the turn of the century. In 1896 lumberman Duncan D. McMillan was the first to go belly-up after backing his three sons, John H., Dan, and Will, in a monumentally unsuccessful Texas grain-buying business patterned after W. W. Cargill's operations in the Midwest. The McMillans were utterly and completely ruined, and John went to work for his father-in-law, W. W. Cargill.

The first of John and Edna Cargill MacMillan's two sons, John Hugh, Jr., had been born in Fort Worth in 1895, the year in which family fortunes reached their nadir. In one of the ironies of the family history, the little boy's grandfather, Duncan D. McMillan, and his father, John, Sr., were divested of their entire assets on his first birthday by a trust headed by W. W. Cargill. Well before John, Jr. grew to manhood, however, the situation would be reversed, and MacMillan interests would control the grain company W. W. Cargill had founded.

The MacMillan story was getting more interesting all the time! Having only brought the family up to the turn of the century, we also already had enough manuscript and terrific pictures to fill a large volume, so we decided to make this a two-volume history. We sent Volume 1 to the printer and commenced work on Volume 2, which begins in 1903, when W. W. Cargill transferred John H. MacMillan to Minnesota to manage the Minneapolis end of his far-flung businesses. The year 1903 was a good starting point for the second book. It was pretty much all uphill from here for the MacMillans.

John H. was the right man for the right job at the right time. He had learned valuable lessons he never forgot from

John, Sr. and Edna
Cargill MacMillan

the debacle in Texas, and he was fresh from managing a sawmill operation for W. W. Cargill in Arkansas. The John H. MacMillans moved into the exclusive Loring Park neighborhood of Minneapolis and took their place among the city's new elite, wealthy families connected with the city's prosperous lumber, grain, and milling industries. John, Jr. attended Emerson Grammar School where one of his classmates was J. Paul Getty.

When W. W. Cargill died, desperately overextended, in 1909, the pendulum of fortune began to swing toward a MacMillan hegemony. W. W.'s eldest son, William Samuel Cargill, was the heir apparent to his father's holdings, but he had talked W. W. into financing a mammoth irrigation scheme in Montana that nearly brought down the house of Cargill. Shunning William Samuel, a creditors' committee elected John MacMillan to head the Cargill Elevator Company and its subsidiaries. John MacMillan immediately moved Cargill headquarters from La Crosse to offices in the Security Bank Building in Minneapolis.

It was a whole new ball game at Cargill. Formerly, the company had pursued an aggressive policy of expansion, adding to its holdings year by year. Forced now to assume a

John H. MacMillan, Jr.

conservative stance, Cargill had to have every outlay approved by the banks, and there was no margin for taking risks. The whole family tightened their belts to eliminate unnecessary expenditures, and John H. himself counted every penny, sometimes writing creditors concerning discrepancies that amounted to less than a dollar. Thanks to his vigilance, Cargill paid its creditors in full in 1916.

"We cleaned up the estate on Saturday exactly as per the plan which I showed you when you were home," he wrote on July 5 to John, Jr., who was drilling with the Yale Battalion at Camp Summerall in Pennsylvania. America was on the brink of war. German U-boats had torpedoed and sunk the Cunard liner *Lusitania* off the Irish coast the previous May, with the loss of more than 1,100 civilian lives, 128 of them American.

When the United States declared war on Germany in April 1917, twenty-one-year-old John, Jr. skipped graduation exercises at Yale to enroll in the First Officers' Training Camp at Fort Snelling, Minnesota. After graduating from the thirteen-week crash program as a captain of field artillery, he was assigned to General Stephen Foote's 163rd Field Artillery Brigade at Camp Dodge in central Iowa. Shipped to France in August 1918, at age twenty-two, John, Jr. was promoted to major, reportedly the youngest one in the United States Army. At the front, as General Foote's adjutant, John, Jr. met General Pershing; behind the lines, he and General Foote socialized with the local gentry, who entertained them at some of the finest country houses in southern France.

John H. MacMillan, Jr.

John, Jr.'s wartime experiences shaped the rest of his life. He later built a French chateau-style residence for his family in what became the MacMillan compound outside Minneapolis in Orono on Lake Minnetonka, and he put organizational management techniques learned in the army to good use in the family business. Following World War II, when he moved Cargill's world headquarters from downtown Minneapolis to the Rand mansion on Lake Minnetonka, where top officers could work more creatively and efficiently in a secluded think-tank type of environment, he was emulating General Pershing, who had directed American field operations from a country house at Chaumont.

John, Jr., W. Duncan MacMillan's father, was actually the most interesting character in this whole family drama. After living at home with his parents and remaining single into his early thirties, in March 1927, while visiting his Aunt Emma Hanchette (Edna's sister) in California, he fell head over heels in love with a red-haired tennis player named Marion Hamilton Dickson Ehrhorn, the thirty-four-year-old widow of a Bolivian tin mining heir. John, Jr. had known Marion just one week when he asked her to marry him and she accepted. After setting a wedding date for May, John, Jr. returned to work in Cargill's Minneapolis office, and the two continued their brief courtship by mail. It might be better, he advised her in one letter, if they kept quiet about her being Catholic and let some of his relatives find out gradually that she was not "a good Presbyterian."

An amateur meteorologist (who thought he had discovered a tenth planet he named "Hellangone"), engineer, and inventor as well as a businessman, John, Jr. has been described as a "one-man band," who supplied the creative energy that gave Cargill a leg up on its competitors. In 1930, going out on a limb with his father's blessing and technical help from colleague Frank Neilson, he had built a radically new type of large-bin elevator with a suspended roof at Omaha that revolutionized grain elevator construction. The next year at Albany, New York, he built the same elevator, only bigger; it

Marion Hamilton Dickson Ehrhorn MacMillan on her wedding day

was the world's largest terminal elevator and the showpiece of the rapidly expanding Cargill Company.

John, Jr. headed Cargill from 1936 until his death in 1960. His beloved *Carmac*, the company's "inspection vessel" was the largest American yacht on the high seas, and his passion for boats begot Cargill's shipbuilding division. During World War II, two thousand miles from the sea, Cargill, Inc. built eighteen tankers for the navy and four tow boats for the army at Port Cargill in Minnesota.

Obsessed with his health and his cholesterol levels as he grew older, John, Jr., put himself on a rigid salt-free rice diet that left him looking like Mahatma Gandhi. He was a few days short of his sixty-fifth birthday when he collapsed at his dining room table in Orono, devastated by the news that his lifelong friend and cousin, Howard McMillan, had passed away suddenly the night before from a heart attack. There had been hard feelings between the two men over a stock deal, and John, Jr. now had no chance to make things right. Following three brain operations, unconscious and with a tube in his brain, John, Jr. was flown in a navy plane to Duke University Medical Center in Durham, North Carolina, where he died two days before Christmas, 1960.

Volume 2 of *MacGhillemhaoil* was on the press in early March 1992, but it was not a happy time for Duncan. His wife Sally had been diagnosed with cancer and the prognosis was not good. The doctors would never find Sally's primary cancer. Duncan dedicated Volume 2 to her:

With Duncan MacMillan and MacGillemhaoil, Volume 2

For Sally,
whose tremendous strength and
fortitude are an inspiration to me.
I am what I am because of her.

Duncan had been very eager for this book, asking me every time I saw him when it would be ready, so the day that it was, I wanted to present it to him in some special way. As soon as I heard from Gregor Campbell that he had books bound and ready to be picked up, I called a Scottish piper friend of mine and asked him to please meet me at the Cargill Office Center in the early afternoon. I also called Sally and invited her to come to Duncan's office. The plan was to surprise Duncan when he came in after lunch, and we did!

Duncan was no sooner in his office than he heard Scottish bagpipes coming down the hall. Peering out, he saw the piper advancing, and behind him, me carrying *the* book. In Scottish fashion, we piped in Volume 2 of *MacGhillemhaoil*. Duncan loved it, and we also caused a stir throughout the Cargill Office Center. Duncan's secretary, Mary Manville, had arranged for refreshments. Best of all, Duncan's dedication was a surprise for Sally.

While completing Volume 2 of *MacGhillemhaoil*, I had also completed the manuscript for a coffee-table book about artist Francis Lee Jaques for a publisher in South Carolina. This was another one of those projects that I couldn't turn down. Jaques was the first, and, for my money, the best of the many Minnesota wildlife painters. The Jaques book was conceived as part of a series about wildlife artists called "Masters of the Wild." Some of the other artists included Bob Kuhn, Robert Abbett, Guy Coheleach, and David Maass.

I knew quite a bit about wildlife art in general and Jaques in particular. I was writing a regular art column for *Sporting Classics* magazine for editor Chuck Wechsler, whom I had met years earlier in St. Paul when he was editor of *The Minnesota Volunteer*, an environmental magazine published by the Minnesota Department of Natural Resources. *Sporting Classics* was located in Camden, South Carolina, and had some connection to the publisher of the "Masters of the Wild" series. Chuck was editing these books and had been the one who asked me to write the Jaques book. In 1982 I had written magazine articles about Jaques for both *Sporting Classics* and *Twin Cities* magazines on the occasion of a major retrospective show of Jaques's paintings and drawings at the James Ford Bell Museum of Natural History at the

University of Minnesota in Minneapolis.

The Jaques book was a joy to write. "Lee," as he preferred to be called, was an innovative, mild-mannered genius who became one of this country's finest wildlife painters. Largely self-taught, he developed a fluid, lyrical style, though rooted in Impressionism, that was distinctly his own. His deep and abiding preoccupation with the wilderness world enabled him to know and understand his subject material in a way that few artists ever can, but he prided himself on never being a feather painter. "I never intended to produce giant Kodachromes," he once said.

After making his living first as a taxidermist, then as a railroad fireman, stoking giant steam engines, Lee Jaques was almost forty when he was first hired as a museum artist

Lee Jaques painting a background for Congo Forest diorama at American Museum of Natural History

in 1924. During the next eighteen years at the American Museum of Natural History in New York, he painted some fifty large diorama backgrounds, his best-known work, each one a masterpiece. His job entailed some exciting field work. In 1928, for instance, he accompanied a six-month AMNH expedition to the Arctic on the fa-

Canvasbacks and Swans *by F. L. Jaques*

mous schooner *Effie M. Morrissey* to collect materials for sea bird and walrus dioramas. The *Morrissey's* skipper was the legendary Captain Bob Bartlett, who had piloted Admiral Robert Peary's ship on his successful trip to the North Pole in 1909.

As an easel painter, in his off-time and after he retired, Lee Jaques charted new directions for wildlife art. He was the first American bird artist to put his subjects *into* the landscape, instead of merely against it. He was concerned with the total composition, not just portraiture, and his paintings combine elegance and beauty of design with technical accuracy. He painted songbirds on occasion, but he excelled at waterfowl. "The larger birds are more paintable," he said. "They have more character."

Myself, I prefer Jaques's paintings of large mammals, which are reminiscent of those of Carl Rungius, the German artist who crossed the Atlantic in 1894 at the age of twenty-five and became a master painter of the great game animals of

Caribou on Ice *by F. L. Jaques*

western North America. One of my favorite Jaques canvases, *Caribou on Ice*, owned by the Bell Museum of Natural History in Minneapolis, depicts a band of caribou on frozen Gunflint Lake in northern Minnesota. A few years ago Charlie and I were lucky enough to trade a couple of Philip R. Goodwin sketches we owned for a superb Jaques painting of an elk.

In a third arena, Lee Jaques illustrated more than forty books, many of them with his crisp black-and-white scratch-board drawings. He was a pioneer in this technique early in his career, and his style is often copied. With his wife, writer

Florence Page Jaques, he collaborated on several books with scratchboard drawings that have become wilderness classics, including perennial favorites *Canoe Country* and *Snowshoe Country*.

Charlie and I first met Lee and Florence Jaques one winter evening in the 1960s when they were living in the St. Paul suburb of North Oaks. Before it was subdivided in the early 1950s, North Oaks had been railroad builder James J. Hill's summer stock farm. After Lee retired from the American Museum in New York, he and Florence bought one of the first lots and built the only home they ever owned. Framed by two splendid oaks, their low, pink brick and white-shingled house nestled behind a small hill that rose up between North Mallard and South Mallard ponds.

Charlie had known Lee by reputation for decades, having first seen his illustrations as a teenager when he worked in the gun department at the old Kennedy Brothers Arms Company in St. Paul. Hanging from the balcony overlooking the book department were enlargements of several Jaques drawings from *Canoe Country*. Charlie spent part of his paycheck to purchase his first Jaques book. Now that he was curator of exhibits at the Science Museum in St. Paul, he hoped to persuade Lee to paint some diorama backgrounds for a new biology hall.

This was not possible, Lee told him. He was in his seventies by then and only doing easel painting. But he did readily agree to lend a carload of his paintings to the museum for an exhibition that Charlie organized. I say carload, because Charlie later picked up the canvases in our Chevy Nomad station wagon. Lee helped him pack the paintings between pieces of cardboard he cut from the box for a new refrigerator that Jaques had recently purchased.

Many of the canvases Lee showed us that first night at

his home are now at the James Ford Bell Museum, among them *The Road West* with its single magpie, and *The Jackrabbit*, its subject silhouetted against a cloud-filled sky. Most of the paintings were for sale, some for as little as $350. The most expensive was *Caribou on Ice*, which hung in the couple's dining area. Lee would have sold it to us for $750. I'm guessing it would now bring in excess of $50,000.

We couldn't afford a painting on Charlie's meager museum salary, but Lee also had scratchboard drawings that he brought out when we asked. These had been used for book illustrations and he apologized because some of them were soiled with printers' smudges. But we were welcome to take our pick, he said, and we did, at prices beginning at five and ten dollars. Lee also still had a few of his duck stamp prints. These were thirty-five dollars.

In 1940 Lee Jaques had been one of the first artists selected to design the annual Federal Duck Stamp. Today's duck stamp artists issue thousands of prints of their winning entries, but Lee was more cautious. He published a first edition of about thirty prints. After these sold, he did a second edition, also about thirty. Collectors snapped up these as well, so he threw caution to the wind and increased his third edition to about two hundred. The last time I checked, a third edition Jaques duck stamp print was quoted at $5,000; a first edition was going for $13,000. What price beauty, indeed!

The Jaques book with its gorgeous illustrations in living color was going to be my most beautiful trade book by far, and I was eagerly awaiting its publication when I learned that this wasn't going to happen. At least not anytime soon. The publisher had had a great idea in his "Masters of the Wild" series, but these large, full-color books were also very expensive to produce. With the Jaques title scheduled to be number seven in the series, he went bankrupt at number six.

Federal Duck Stamp design, 1940

So I had the manuscript for a great book but no publisher. Shelving it for the time being, I considered the possibility of one day starting a small non-profit press to publish extravagant books like the Jaques book would have been. I would concentrate on Minnesota subjects, I decided, and the non-profit aspect was important because such an organization could seek out and accept tax-deductible contributions from individuals and organizations to offset publication costs. I didn't want what had happened to the South Carolina publisher to happen to me. Charlie gave me my first dollar, which I still have, for what I was already calling the Afton Historical Society Press. I wanted this organization to sound official, and there actually *is* an Afton Historical Society.

Meanwhile, Duncan MacMillan and I were exploring options for publishing a trade edition of his family book. We met and talked with literary agent Jonathan Lazear, but we couldn't reach an agreement concerning content. "As you know," Jonathon wrote in one letter to me, "when the average American picks up a book about the rich and powerful, they want to read about the dirt. They're not as interested these days in an uplifting and beautiful story like the MacMillan saga."

For a time we signed on with literary agent Pam Bernstein at the William Morris agency in New York. The publishers to whom she sent our materials picked their words more carefully but said much the same thing. Senior Editor Thomas Miller at HarperCollins wrote: "This is a fascinating story, but ultimately we weren't sure there would be a large enough audience for the book." Senior Editor Ann Harris at Bantam Books declined "with regret the outline and partial manuscript of the MacMillan family by W. Duncan MacMillan. . . . It is obviously a remarkable family, as is Cargill, Inc.; but . . . our feeling is that the book will not find a wide enough readership for it to be a possibility for the Bantam list."

There was another option, I told Duncan, and that was to start our own press, the non-profit one I had in mind. "If you do decide to self-publish, you could use this book to launch a new Minnesota small press," I wrote in one note to him. "This is a very exciting option, one that could keep you in publishing indefinitely and involved with some truly prestigious projects." Little did we know just how much we actually *could* accomplish at the Afton Historical Society Press!

I was also now hearing from Chuck Wechsler at *Sporting Classics* magazine that he would like to revive the Francis Lee Jaques book project and was looking for a co-publisher. This couldn't have happened at a better time, and I took the idea to Duncan. This was the deal: Chuck would edit, arrange for design, and produce the book from Camden for LiveOak Press, it would be printed and bound in Hong Kong, and we would share equally in the costs, based on the number of books we each wanted.

This was the nudge we had needed. We signed the incorporation papers for the non-profit Afton Historical Society

Press in July 1993. Duncan and I both agreed that *The Shape of Things: The Art of Francis Lee Jaques* was the right first book for our new Minnesota press, and it was. Published in 1994, *The Shape of Things* won both the 1995 Minnesota Book Award for

Best Illustrated Book as well as the 1995 Midwest Independent Publishers Association (MIPA) Award for Best First Book (from a new press).

The Afton Historical Society Press was my dream come true, and I am grateful every day to Duncan MacMillan for making it a reality. We are an autonomous organization, not affiliated with the Afton Historical Society, except that they were good enough to let us use their name. We began with no staff. I was named publisher and director, Duncan was chairman and president. We didn't have an office, but I signed up for a second-floor room in the old lumberyard building in Afton, which was being renovated for office space. For the time being, I would continue to work at home.

I brought to this new Afton Press a long list of books I wanted to write and publish that I was continually adding to, but I also realized that I would never be able to write all of these books myself. Now I had a better idea: I would find the best qualified authors to write the books I had in mind. The press of my dreams would produce beautiful books that also met high standards of scholarship and literary value.

One of the first books I wanted the new Afton Press to publish would showcase the spectacular collection of Seth Eastman watercolors owned by the James J. Hill Reference Library in St. Paul. I had written about this collection many years earlier for *American History Illustrated* magazine and had since imagined being able to publish the kind of full-color book that would do them justice. So in the fall of 1993, I called on the library's director and asked her for permission to photograph the paintings and to reproduce them in a book. Much to my surprise, she said no.

I had gone in thinking the Hill Library would be more than happy to cooperate in a venture that would make available to a wide audience the most significant source of information we have about Indian life in Minnesota in the 1840s. Seth Eastman was a career army officer and a talented artist assigned to Fort Snelling on the Minnesota frontier who set out to preserve a visual record of Indian life which was then undergoing rapid change. Unlike some of his contemporaries, including George Catlin and Karl Bodmer, Captain Eastman did not fall into the trap of romanticizing the Indians, and he is widely appreciated today for his ethnographic detail.

Indians Traveling *by Seth Eastman*

Eastman's long-term military residency among the Indians enabled him to become familiar not only with their colorful external trappings but also with the whole complex fabric of Indian culture. His portfolio included scenes of winter villages and temporary summer encampments, courting and marriage customs, and Indian burial grounds; Indians making maple sugar, protecting their cornfields from birds, spearing fish, and gathering wild rice; the menstrual lodge, the manner in which

Dakota Burial Ground *by Seth Eastman*

Dakota women sat, and the medicine men concocting potions and ministering to the sick. Monumentally important as American art, Eastman's paintings are also vital to our understanding of Dakota and Ojibwe life in pre-territorial Minnesota.

The Hill Library didn't want an Eastman book because it didn't want to call attention to the works, the largest extant collection of Eastman watercolors. The paintings had been in the library since its completion in 1920, and before

Gathering Wild Rice *by Seth Eastman*

Guarding the Cornfields *by Seth Eastman*

that, in Hill's personal library at his Summit Avenue home in St. Paul. Sometime between the time when Charlie photographed them for the *American History Illustrated* article and when I requested permission to photograph them for a book, their status had changed from library collections to "portfolio assets." With the boom in the western art market in recent years, their value had increased significantly, and they were kept locked in a safe on the library's fourth floor. The Hill didn't have enough staff to handle requests to see the paintings, I was told, and we would not be given permission to photograph them, period.

I couldn't walk away from this book, however. It was simply too important, and when I couldn't get the cooperation of the library director, I began lobbying board members and Hill's great-grandchildren, one of whom, Sheila ffolliott, was chair of the department of art history at George Mason University in Fairfax, Virginia. When Sheila came to the Twin Cities to present a program at the Minneapolis Institute of Arts, I was in the audience and afterwards went up and introduced myself.

Sheila promised to see what she could do, and she and her husband, Shepard Krech, the director of the Haffenreffer Museum of Anthropology at Brown University, became staunch advocates for our project. It never occurred to me that Afton might not ever gain access to the Eastman paintings, but for now the project was in limbo.

Duncan also wanted us to do a gardening book. He was thinking of his wife Sally and her passion for gardening. Sally was a third-generation gardener whose great love of flowers and trees and shrubs had been passed down to her by her mother and grandmother, both of whom had had beautiful gardens in the East. Sally had some of the loveliest gardens in Minnesota, and she was the historian for the Lake Minnetonka Garden Club. Since there had never been a history of Minnesota gardens, that's what we decided to do: *Minnesota Gardens: An Illustrated History*.

With a little coaxing, Sally agreed to write the foreword, and the two of us had great fun planning this book—over lunch in Wayzata, over lunch in Stillwater, at my house, and at hers. Sally knew a great deal about various Minnesota gardens—who had the best ones, who used to have the best ones, and the professional gardeners behind some of them. Sadly, Sally was in the last stages of cancer by then and died a few months before *Minnesota Gardens* was published in late 1995.

Minnesota Gardens was written by Susan Davis Price, a reference librarian at the University of St. Thomas in St. Paul, as well as a master gardener, who was writing garden articles for both local and national magazines. We learned about Susan from the Minnesota Horticultural Society. In the course of her research for *Minnesota Gardens*, Susan collected some really remarkable historic photographs throughout the state. We augmented these with photographs by a number of outstanding Minnesota photographers including

D. R. Martin, Lynn Steiner, and my husband Charlie.

If all went well, and we could obtain permission to photograph and reproduce the Eastman paintings—I was still counting on this—Afton would publish four books in 1995:

1. *Seth Eastman: A Portfolio of North American Indians*

2. *Dahcotah; or, Life and Legends of the Sioux* (by Mary Henderson Eastman with illustrations by Seth Eastman. Mary Eastman was Seth's wife, who accompanied him to the Minnesota frontier. We planned to reprint *Dahcotah*, which had originally been published in Philadelphia in 1849, as a companion volume to *Seth Eastman: A Portfolio of North American Indians*.)

3. *Minnesota Gardens: An Illustrated History*

4. *Stillwater: Minnesota's Birthplace* (a revised edition of my earlier book for Johnston Publishing)

It was the best year of my life, no question, with the Afton Historical Society Press a reality, our first book at the printer, and several more in the works. Or so I thought at the time, not knowing that life was about to take a terrible, terrible turn for our family.

8

No Middle Ground

WHAT BEGAN as the best year of my life turned out to be the worst. It is hard to imagine anything more horrible than what our family experienced on a cold day in late November 1993.

I was in Florida earlier that month when the first press proofs for *The Shape of Things* began arriving from Hong Kong. A large bundle was delivered to my mother's house in Hollywood where I was caring for her. Mom had broken her pelvis while riding a horse. She was seventy-eight years old and hadn't been on a horse for years, but my brother D. J. (now a Florida law enforcement officer who lives with his family in rural Fort Lauderdale) had asked her if she would like to ride one of his. Silly boy! The horse had given Mom a terrific jouncing. By the time I arrived in Florida several weeks later, she had undergone two operations to piece her together again. She was convalescing at home in a hospital bed in her "Florida room," which looks out on her patio

My daughter Patty with my mother, Betty Condon

155

and pool.

It was wonderful being with my mother. She was a good and easy patient, and we enjoyed our time together. In between cooking meals and cleaning up, I sat outside on the patio (at the glass-topped wrought iron table that had been our breakfast room table when we all lived together on Lake Harriet in Minneapolis) and read page proofs. The weather had already turned wintry in Minnesota, so the Florida sunshine was a bonus. My sister Colleen arrived after a week's time to take over with Mom, and since she too lives in Florida and we only see each other every few years, I cherished every minute of the partial day we had together. I spent my last night in Florida at D. J.'s house with D. J. and his wife Lee (who is also a Florida law enforcement officer) and their two beautiful dark-haired daughters, Kelly and Erin. A week earlier, I'd been reluctant to come to Florida—I hated flying and was actually scared to death of it, and I didn't know if I was really up to caring for my mother, but D. J. had asked me to, and the week had worked out wonderfully. D. J. took me to the airport to fly home on Sunday afternoon, November 21.

Charlie met my plane in St. Paul, and we ate a late lunch at the Lexington Restaurant on Grand Avenue. I've always been partial to the "Lex," which is paneled in dark oak and is just five blocks from where I grew up on the corner of Hague and Lexington. That evening my daughter Jane called me to see that I had made it home safely. We were in the habit of talking to each other every day on the telephone, and we had some catching up to do. Jane and her husband, Jim Neumann, and their twenty-one-month-old son, Jonny, lived about fifteen minutes away from us in rural Hudson, Wisconsin. I loved having them close by.

The next morning, Monday, Jane called me from the mortgage banking company where she worked. Thursday would be Thanksgiving, and for the second year in a row, Jane had invited the whole family to her house. I was going to prepare the turkey, but I would cook it at home, I told her. "Do you think I have enough sweet potatoes?" Jane asked me; she had two cans. We talked about potatoes and rolls and cranberries and sweet pickles.

That afternoon Charlie and I did some errands in St. Paul and afterwards stopped for a light supper at the Green Mill on Grand Avenue. While waiting for our meal, we browsed some of the free newspapers we had picked up from racks in front of the restaurant. One paper contained the tragic story of a young father who had recently driven his bicycle into a telephone pole near the St. Paul Cathedral and was now par-

My daughter Jane and me

alyzed. How very lucky we were, I commented to Charlie. We had four grown children, all of them married and happy. Mary Sue had been married just six weeks earlier. Jane had been her matron of honor. We had so much to be thankful for.

That evening at home, I was still feeling lucky, *very* lucky to be doing the work I liked best—making books. I was pouring over final page proofs for *The Shape of Things* at the kitchen table when I was startled by a sharp knock on the front door. It was about nine o'clock, and Charlie had gone up to bed early with a book, so I went into the front hall and turned on the outdoor lights. Outside I could see Jim Zeller, a longtime family friend, who was also our son-in-law Jim Neumann's employer. Zeller was sheet-white, and I knew instantly that something was terribly wrong.

"Get Charlie," Zeller told me as I let him in, and I ran up the stairs, my mind racing as Charlie grabbed for his robe. There had been an automobile accident, I knew it, and either Jane or Jim was dead. Somebody was dead!

Downstairs, the three of us went into the living room. "Jim, what's the matter?" I pleaded. "Jane's been shot," he said. "How is she?" I gasped—but I already knew. My heart felt like it had been ripped from my chest. "She's dead," he said quietly. "No! No! No!" I can still hear myself screaming. "She can't be! Not Jane! Not Jane! She can't be."

The police were at the Neumann residence, Zeller said. It appeared that Jane had been shot by an intruder, possibly a hunter. Jim Neumann had come home from work and found her in their lower-level family room, dead of a gunshot wound to the head.

Two days later, on Wednesday afternoon, Washington County Attorney Dick Arney, one of Charlie's fishing buddies, came to see Charlie and me. He had some news we weren't going to want to hear, he said. Taking us into Charlie's library, he told us that Jim Neumann had changed his story. The truth was that Jane had committed suicide, Arney said. She had shot herself with a shotgun. I didn't believe this and I never would. I had spoken to Jane the morning of the day she died, I said. Besides, how could she have killed herself with a shotgun? Arney said he didn't have many details. The one thing he knew was that the police now believed that Jane had killed herself.

Neumann had changed his story after being caught in a lie by Jim Zeller, who was driving him to St. Paul to buy a suit for Jane's funeral. En route, Zeller had stopped for gas and picked up a newspaper. The story it contained about Jane's death stated that Neumann had called 911 at 6:18 p.m.

My daughter Jane Ellen Johnston Neumann

This didn't make sense to Zeller, who had asked Neumann for a ride home from work in St. Paul on the afternoon Jane died. Neumann had dropped Zeller off in Zeller's driveway about 5:45. The Neumanns lived only five minutes away, so what had gone on in that missing half hour, Zeller wanted to know. Neumann was reluctant to talk about it, Zeller would tell us later, but Neumann finally "admitted" that Jane had committed suicide.

Zeller turned the car around, forgetting the suit errand, and took Neumann to see attorney Jack Walsh in Stillwater. Walsh told them that Neumann might be charged and jailed. Since the next day was Thanksgiving, Zeller went next to a bank and withdrew five thousand dollars should Neumann need bail money. Zeller and Neumann then proceeded to the St. Croix County Government Center in Hudson where police took Neumann's revised statement.

Neumann now said he had come home from work, smelled gunpowder, and found Jane dead of a *self-inflicted* gunshot wound. She had apparently made a hole in the wall separating the family room from the laundry room, he said, and pushed the barrel of a shotgun through it from the laundry room side. She then stood on the family room side of the wall and pulled the trigger with fishing line. After finding her, Neumann said, he had altered the scene to preserve her reputation and spare her family the pain of finding out that she had killed herself.

To make it appear that, instead, she had been killed by an intruder, Neumann said he had

1. picked up the gun (using a pair of Jane's gloves so as not to leave fingerprints), wrapped it in garbage bags (which he weighted down with screws and such to be sure the package would sink), driven with it several miles to the St. Croix River (where he parked and ran several hundred

yards up onto the westbound I-94 bridge during rush-hour traffic), and thrown it off the bridge.

2. found Jane's suicide note, read it, burned it, swept up the ashes, and flushed them down the toilet.

3. hung a picture (it turned out to be a charcoal sketch of a bobcat Charlie had made and given to Jane and Jim) over the hole in the wall that the gun had come through.

4. pushed in the front door with his *shoulder* to make it look like the house had been broken into. (Police photos would show that the door was *kicked* in below the doorknob.)

Then he called 911. On the audio tape of that call, Neumann is crying hysterically. He reports that his wife is dead and his son is missing. In fact, Jonny was with his day-care provider in Hudson. Jim had taken him there himself that morning, after Jane had already gone to work.

The police believed Neumann's story. He wouldn't need any bail money. They had already come to their own conclusion that the crime scene had been "altered." Jim was charged with "obstruction of justice" for tampering with the crime scene. At his trial several weeks later, he would be fined something less than $5,000, the cost of the "unnecessary" police investigation. He would be able to pay this amount after collecting approximately $116,000 from one of the insurance policies he held on Jane's life.

On Thanksgiving Day, numbed by grief, I baked the turkey that I was to have taken to Jane's house. I didn't bother with stuffing. We wouldn't be having a traditional sit-down dinner. Everybody pretty much just made sandwiches whenever they were hungry. The rest of our children had come home and were staying with us—Patty and her husband, Tom Gnojek, and their two little boys, Damon and Dylan, from Utah; Chuck and his wife, Kelly, with their baby, Sam, from Minneapolis; and Mary Sue, from Hudson, Wisconsin.

The long days of agony were taking their toll. Everybody was exhausted. We couldn't fathom what had happened or why. Charlie was very distraught and stayed in bed all that day. He had already had one heart attack a few years earlier, and we worried that he might have another. I called his physician who prescribed something over the phone. Charlie said he didn't think he would be able to attend the funeral the next morning.

On Friday morning, Charlie got up very angry, got dressed, and said that he was going to Jane's funeral. "Jane didn't kill herself," he told me. Of course, she hadn't, I knew that. I saw that he was drawing strength from his anger and I called up my own deep well of anger to get me through this terrible day. We drove to the church together, and once inside, I planted myself beside the door. Embracing people as they came in, I told them, "Jane didn't do this." All of my siblings were there—Colleen, Tom, Mary Ellen, O'Ann, and D. J. Except for Tom, who lives in Stillwater, Minnesota, they had all flown up from Florida where they were living. Friends whom we hadn't seen in years came to share this sad time with us. Almost everybody was fighting back tears, many people wept openly.

Church bells pealed twelve o'clock as we trudged through fresh snow behind Jane's casket from the small church to the higher burying ground. I remember particularly the smell of evergreen from ancient pines that had been planted there by some of the first settlers in this valley. The Lutheran pastor (who had been kind enough to bring a portable crib to our house for one of our visiting grandchildren) said a few words. One by one, those closest to Jane placed single white roses on her coffin. A bagpiper in kilts on a nearby hill played "Going Home." It was more beautiful, and more terrible, than anything I could have imagined.

Two officers came to see us the day after Jane's funeral. I had called them and asked them to come, while all of our children were at home, and our family talked at length about the impossibility of the suicide scenario. Jane was a happy young mother who adored her young son. Mary Sue had been talking about buying the lot next door to Jane and Jim because the two girls were best friends and wanted to raise their children together. Where did Jane get a gun and what really became of it? (It would never turn up in the river, which was dragged several times by expert divers.)

We didn't know it, and wouldn't know it for several months, but the case had already been closed. The police were just hearing us out. By March, however, I finally realized that they were doing absolutely nothing, and I phoned Dick Arney. Could I come up to see him at his office in Stillwater? Mary Sue went with me and we told Dick that we didn't believe Jane's death was a suicide. He was surprised to hear that the gun supposedly had been propped up in an adjacent room and that Jane was supposed to have killed herself by pulling on a piece of fishing line attached to the trigger. He hadn't known about this, he said. He told us that when people kill themselves with a shotgun they usually put their big toe in the trigger. What we were telling him sounded like Jane had been ambushed, he said. Dick also told us that the case was indeed closed and that because it was, we were entitled to see the district attorney's files in Hudson. Mary Sue and I went there immediately from Dick's office.

What we read in the district attorney's files confirmed our thinking that Jane had been murdered, and I talked next with Duncan MacMillan. Duncan had told me from the time of Jane's death that he would do anything he could to help our family. Now he suggested that we hire a criminal attorney to look into Jane's death, and he ended up retaining

Mark Gherty in Hudson for us. Duncan placed the initial call to Mark while I was in his office. Mark knew about the case, he said, and would be glad to represent us. No one has ever had a better attorney.

From the spring of 1994 until November 1995, two years after Jane's death, Mark helped me conduct our own private investigation. What we uncovered was a very complicated plot that told us, without a doubt, that Jim Neumann had been behind Jane's death. We turned our findings over to both local and state authorities and implored them to bring charges. When they refused to act, on the second anniversary of Jane's death, the last possible date on which we could do so, we filed a wrongful death suit against Neumann in St. Croix County, Wisconsin.

We were following the lead of Ron Goldman's parents who were suing O. J. Simpson in California. Nicole Brown Simpson and Ron Goldman had been killed a year after Jane died, and I had watched some of the O. J. trial on television. What about my own daughter? I had thought at the time. There was no spotlight on her death. How could people in Jane's own community be interested in murders that had taken place in California and not care that this beautiful young woman had been murdered in their midst?

It would take another year and a half before our case came to trial in St. Croix County Court in June 1997. When it did, the TV cameras were there en masse. This was the first time a criminal case had been heard in civil court in Wisconsin. Susan Spencer of CBS covered the trial for *48 Hours*, which filmed every minute of the seven-day trial for a one-hour program that has aired many times. When the twelve jurors came back, after being out for just a few hours on the evening of June 17, they were unanimous in their decision. Jane had been murdered, they said, and her husband had done it. (Because this was a civil, not a criminal, case, we hadn't needed a unanimous decision, only ten out of twelve.)

Most people in the packed courtroom that night expected that Jim Neumann would then be arrested. Officers had been placed at the courtroom doors, and a doorway leading directly to jail from the courtroom had been cleared of television gear. Mark Gherty and Jim's attorney next met with authorities in chambers for what seemed an

Susan Spencer interviewing me and Charlie outside the St. Croix County courthouse for the television news show, 48 Hours.

eternity. Finally Mark came out, very angry, and announced: "You can all go home, folks. The sheriff has decided that Jim Neumann is free to go."

Neumann and his second wife, Heather, walked out of the courtroom and quickly flew back to the state of Washington where they were living, and he is still a free man.

There were positive results from this trial, however. Judge Eric Lundell, who heard the case, ordered Jane's death certificate changed from suicide to homicide. Because of this change, her case was reopened and remains open in St. Croix County. Authorities obviously still don't believe they have a strong enough case with which to charge Jim, but we have to believe that they one day will. Also, because of the official change from suicide to homicide, the proceeds from several additional insurance policies on Jane's life became available. Jim was the beneficiary, but he declined to accept payment, stating that he still believed his wife had committed suicide, so the proceeds went to Jane and Jim's son Jonny. This money has been deposited in a trust fund set up for him by Mark Gherty in St. Croix County.

It breaks our hearts that Jonny remains with Jim Neumann and his wife Heather, who now also have two children of their own. Our primary goal all along was to protect Jonny and to gain custody of him, which we have been unable to do. Without our knowledge, Heather was able to adopt Jonny in Washington. At one point we hired an attorney there to pursue our grandparents' rights. He told us that even if Jim were arrested and sent to prison, Washington would uphold Heather's step-parent rights and we would have very little chance of gaining custody of Jonny.

That I managed to get through those dark days following Jane's death, that everyone in our family did, was due in large part to the support we received from family and friends. Beyond that, however, the Afton Historical Society Press has played a large part these past years in keeping me sane. I'm grateful every day that I have satisfying and consuming work that occupies my mind and feeds my spirit.

In December, less than three weeks after Jane died, the Afton Historical Society Press moved into its first office, a single room on the second floor of the former lumberyard building in Afton. Our furnishings amounted to one large desk, one computer stand, one small round "conference" table, four office chairs on rollers, and one filing cabinet, all of them borrowed from Cargill's "attic." I brought in some of Charlie's paintings and framed prints to hang on the walls. Mary Sue started working with me part-time, and it was truly a momentous day when our first book, *The Shape of Things*, arrived from the printer in February 1994.

This book is very special to me for a number of reasons, but besides the obvious ones—that it is a terrifically good-looking book and that it was the first book published by

Afton—I've always considered it to be "Jane's book." The day after she died, I called Chuck Wechsler in South Carolina and asked him to please include this dedication: "In memory of my beloved Jane Ellen." Just about a year later, I was thinking about Jane and fighting back tears the night I walked to the stage at the Minnesota Book Awards to accept my first award for this book. I was still too reticent to say anything more than "thank you," but I was thinking, "This is for you, Jane."

Mary Sue and I solicited orders for this first Afton book by mailing postcards about *The Shape of Things* to our former Johnston Publishing customers and other prospects. Then we mailed *The Shape of Things* posters and ordering information to librarians at Minnesota schools and libraries, and we contacted newspaper and magazine editors about our new book. We wound up receiving some really terrific publicity. *Ducks Unlimited* magazine did a feature article based on *The Shape of Things*. *Wildlife Art News* said: "Johnston provides a well-written text that complements the strong design, incredible color, and brilliant artistic vision of Francis Lee Jaques." We stayed away from radio and television people. I was pretty sure that I would never want to promote an Afton book on-air. It gave me the heebie-jeebies just thinking about having to speak distinctly and coherently into a microphone.

This new Afton Press still felt a lot like self-publishing. I was still doing the publicity and marketing and calling on bookstores and sometimes delivering books. One difference was that bookseller Steve Anderson, who owns Ross & Haines Old Books in Hudson, Wisconsin, was packing and shipping our books for us. Steve is one of the hardest-working and smartest people I know, and we also use him for proofreading and fact-checking. Steve came close to obtaining a master's degree in history, except that he never wrote his thesis.

The only bookkeeping we did that first year in Afton

was to keep track of the books we sold and to whom, and I did this with a pencil in a ledger. (At the end of the first year I remember being four cents off somewhere and spending hours looking for it; I thought you had to be that precise.) We didn't have any charge card capability. If a customer wanted a book, he or she sent us a check or money order for it. Once a week or so, we mailed all of the checks we had received, along with any invoices for the rent or utilities or printings costs, etc., to Waycrosse, Inc., the MacMillan/Cargill family office at the Cargill Office Center. Waycrosse also handled our payroll, health and property insurance, and taxes. Duncan couldn't have made things much simpler for me.

I didn't spend all day at the office. I still did most of my writing at home, on my own personal computer. We didn't even have a computer at the office, only my old electric type-writer that I'd used for my magazine articles. In the early months of 1994, besides working on the trade edition of the MacMillan book, I was revising my Stillwater book with its splendid period photographs by John Runk. I was also fol-lowing Susan Price's progress with *Minnesota Gardens,* and I certainly hadn't given up on the Seth Eastman book. In fact, we were about to get lucky.

In response to my continued appeals for permission to photograph and publish the paintings, I now heard from act-ing director Richard Slade at the Hill Library. The Eastman watercolors were about to be sold, he wrote. Sotheby's had been called in to appraise the paintings, and the Eastmans would likely be put up at auction in New York. The collection almost certainly would be dispersed, and the library there-fore had no interest in the book we were proposing.

I replied to Mr. Slade, who is also descended from James J. Hill, that *if* the collection were to be dispersed, that this was all the more reason to allow Afton to preserve a visual record of it.

The Eastmans were part of Minnesota's legacy and deserved to be published together in book form. This argument apparently won him over. I learned later that there had also been some Hill family discussions about the importance of the book project. The bottom line was that we would be allowed to photograph the paintings and reproduce them in a book! Mr. Slade made the arrangements.

Our good luck continued when I was able to find the two best possible authors to collaborate on this project with me. The first was Sarah E. Boehme, curator of the Whitney Gallery of Western Art at the Buffalo Bill Historical Center in Cody, Wyoming. Sarah is perhaps the leading Eastman scholar, having written her Ph.D. dissertation about the artist. It just so happened that Sarah was coming to Minneapolis that summer for a meeting of the American Association of University Women (AAUW), so Charlie and I had a chance to meet her and to discuss the Eastman project, in which she became an eager participant.

Sarah wrote the first of the three major sections that comprise *Seth Eastman: A Portfolio of North American Indians*, an essay titled "An Officer and an Illustrator on the Indian Frontier." This introductory essay describes the artist in the context of his times and his role in American art history and is illustrated with work by Eastman and several of his predecessors who painted Indians, including Samuel Seymour, Peter Rindisbacher, and George Catlin. None of these artists, of course, came to know the Indians in the same way that Seth Eastman did; none of them were afforded his unique opportunity of living among them for an extended period of time. In a class by himself, Eastman alone left a body of work that preserves in rich detail much of the complexity of Indian life on the American frontier in the first half of the nineteenth century.

The second section and main body of the book is titled

simply "The Plates." The paintings, most of which are reproduced full size in this 12" x 12" book, are annotated by
Christian F. Feest. Sheila ffolliott put me on to Christian,
telling me that he was the number one scholar of the Dakota
nation. Born and educated in Vienna, Christian was a post-
doctoral fellow at the Smithsonian in the 1970s and also a
Ford Foundation Fellow at the Center of the History of the
American Indian at the Newberry Library in Chicago in the
1980s. Currently professor of anthropology at the University
of Frankfurt, Christian is the author of several books on
Native American subjects and also the editor and publisher
of the *European Review of Native American Studies.*

The two of us corresponded by mail initially, and Christian
also came to Minnesota to see the Eastman paintings. His wonderfully descriptive annotations for the Eastman plates are considerably more than had ever been written previously about
these paintings. Over lunch one day we discussed future projects he would take on for the Afton Historical Society Press,
including *Peoples of the Twilight: European Views of Native
Minnesota, 1823-1865* (which we would publish in 1998).

The third and concluding section of *Seth Eastman*, a
brief biography of the artist I titled "He Chased Indians: The
Soldier Artist's Life," I reserved for myself. I had already
collected every book, every word, that had ever been published about Eastman, and I had wanted to write this biography for years. Besides covering the periods at Fort Snelling,
I discussed Eastman's early life and his years at West Point,
both as a student and later as assistant drawing teacher; his
military service in Florida, fighting Seminoles, and in Texas;
and his parallel career as a ranking American artist. "He
Chased Indians" is illustrated with additional Eastman artwork, including some of his Florida and Texas pictures,
from various museum collections.

Dog Dance of the Dahcotahs *by Seth Eastman*

Sheila ffolliott and Shepard Krech contributed the Preface for *Seth Eastman: A Portfolio of North American Indians*, in which they explained the provenance of these paintings as having belonged to Sheila's great-grandfather, James J. Hill. Like many other wealthy men of his time, Hill collected art, mostly European paintings and sculpture. His family mansion on Summit Avenue in St. Paul included an art gallery, which is almost certainly where he kept the Eastman paintings. Unlike his European paintings, which were framed and hung on the walls, the watercolors were probably laid flat on shelves from which they could be pulled and studied.

One of Hill's granddaughters, Georgiana Slade Reny, recalled for Sheila and Shep a game she had played with her grandfather in the gallery as a child. He "had provided her with a magnifying glass and, proffering some images, challenged her to find certain Indians or Indians engaged in particular tasks. . . . The intricate detail of [the Eastmans] would have provided fertile ground for such explorations, which reminded us both of the game children play today with Martin Handford's books featuring a character called Waldo, whom one tries to find in a sea of activity on each page."

Seth Eastman: A Portfolio of North American Indians was edited by Sally Rubinstein, the resident expert on Native American subjects at the Minnesota Historical Society Press, whom we have used on a free-lance basis for many of our

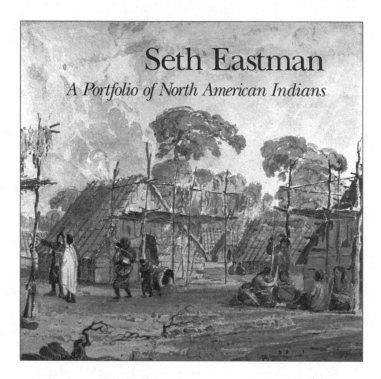

books. It was designed by Barb Arney. I had met Barb after Jane died through Barb's husband Dick. Barb showed me her portfolio, and although she had never designed a book before, we were both confident she could. Barb has since designed many of our award-winning books.

All four of our books for 1995—*Seth Eastman, Dahcotah, Minnesota Gardens*, and *Stillwater* were printed at Litho, Inc. in St. Paul and bound at Midwest Editions in Minneapolis. *Stillwater* and *Minnesota Gardens* were regional titles that we distributed through Bookmen, mainly in Minnesota. Sheila ffolliott had suggested that we contact the University of Washington Press about distributing *Seth Eastman* and *Dahcotah*. This prestigious press, which specializes in publishing and distributing gorgeous and scholarly art books, distributed these Native American titles for us both nationally and internationally.

We received wonderful reviews. Newspapers and magazines across the country reviewed the Eastman books and *Minnesota Gardens*. Former Minnesota Governor Elmer L. Andersen, Minnesota's leading book collector, called *Seth Eastman: A Portfolio of North American Indians* "one of the most important publishing accomplishments of this or any other year."

We were also winning more awards! *Minnesota Gardens* started out by winning the 1996 Minnesota Book Award for Best Minnesota Book and also a 1996 Quill and Trowel Award from the Garden Writers Association of America. The next year it won the 1997 MIPA Award for Best Gardening Book, then went on to capture MIPA's 1997 Best of Show Award!

The Seth Eastman/Hill Library saga came to a very happy conclusion. I had told Duncan MacMillan that the watercolors were about to be sold and that he might wish to consider purchasing this unique collection, which is so important to Minnesota history. He liked this idea.

"In late 1994 the James Jerome Hill Reference Library sold its collection of fifty-six Eastman watercolors . . . to W. Duncan MacMillan of nearby Wayzata," I wrote in an

article for the Sept./Oct. 1996 issue of *American History* magazine. "The library's decision to sell the artworks . . . was predicated on its changing needs [it was moving away from its original mission as a general reference library to focus on business] and budgetary concerns. Proceeds from the sale were added to the library's endowment to support general operations."

Charlie and I picked up the paintings at the Hill Library after Duncan acquired them and safely transported them in our car to the Minneapolis Institute of Arts (MIA), where they have since been on temporary loan. With the Eastman paintings now in private hands, they are more accessible to a wider public than was previously the case, first of all, in our book *Seth Eastman: A Portfolio of North American Indians*. To help launch this book, MIA mounted a partial exhibition of about two dozen of these small paintings.

In 2000 we published *Painting the Dakota: Seth Eastman at Fort Snelling*, our first book for young people, which is illustrated by the MacMillan Collection. We also began production on a second documentary with KTCA-TV (now Twin Cities Public Television or TPT), based on our earlier book, *Seth Eastman: A Portfolio of North American Indians*. We scheduled completion of this documentary to coincide with an exhibition of the MacMillan Collection of Seth Eastman paintings at the Smithsonian's National Museum of the American Indian in New York in the spring of 2001.

"Not everything you touch has to make money," I quoted Duncan as saying about his purchase of the paintings in my *American History* article. "I didn't want to see them broken up and scattered. . . . It seemed to me that if it were possible to acquire the paintings, we would keep them together on behalf of the people of Minnesota."

9

The Coen Brothers' Mother

YOU'VE HEARD OF the famous movie-making Coen brothers, Joel and Ethan? I have to admit that I hadn't when I first met their mother, Rena Neumann Coen. Rena is a leading American art historian, who taught for many years at St. Cloud State in Minnesota, and the person I wanted to write a new book for Afton Press titled *Minnesota Impressionists*. I knew Rena's work from her bicentennial book for the University of Minnesota Press, *Painting and Sculpture in Minnesota, 1820-1914*. I did not know anything about her "boys."

Artist Alexis Jean Fournier

The idea of calling a group of Minnesota artists "Impressionists" was a fresh concept. No one had identified these men and women as such before, and I wondered why not? That's what they were—Nicholas Brewer, Alexis Jean Fournier, Elisabeth Chant, Edwin Dawes, Alexander Grinager, Alice LeDuc, and other Minnesota artists who were directly influenced by the French Impressionists in the period prior to 1940. Like their French counterparts, the Minnesota Impressionists often painted *en plein air*—out-of-doors, and although their individual styles varied considerably, they all painted in an Impressionist mode. By and large they came from pioneer farming families, and they brought to the region a new way of looking at nature and nature's light.

Nicholas Brewer painting out-of-doors

The subject of Minnesota Impressionists appealed to me for personal reasons. Since becoming acquainted with the work of Nicholas Brewer when I was collecting material about his son, Ed Brewer (of Cream of Wheat fame), I had acquired several of his paintings. Coincidentally, one of my Nicholas Brewer paintings, *Mohawk Valley*, once belonged to Rena Coen. This was before I met her. Rena had purchased it at an estate sale and later traded it to Kramer Gallery, where Charlie purchased it for me one year for Christmas. It's a small painting, 8-1/2" x 11-1/2", oil on masonite, with an undated label on the back indicating that it was offered for sale, for $125, at "Loeser's Gallery Thumb Box Exhibition from Members Only of the Salmagundi Club."

I introduced myself to Rena following a public lecture she delivered at the Minneapolis Institute of Arts. This is where I learned that she had once owned *Mohawk Valley*, which she included in her slide show that day. We ended up having lunch at an Indian restaurant across the street from the Institute. Rena liked the idea of "Minnesota Impressionists" and agreed to write the book I envisioned. We met when we could after that, usually over lunch, to discuss how the book was coming along and just because we enjoyed each other's company. One time Rena mentioned that her "boys" made movies. "You probably wouldn't like them [the movies]," she apologized, and I didn't think anymore about it—until *Fargo* was released, and it finally dawned on me who her "boys" were!

Minnesota Impressionists by Rena Neumann Coen opened a new chapter in the history of art in Minnesota. We launched it with an exhibition of the paintings depicted in the book at the Tweed Gallery of Art at the University of Minnesota/Duluth in December 1996. The paintings were borrowed from both museum and private collections. Rena was guest curator for this exhibition, which was organized by Tweed curator Peter Spooner. This  was the first in a continuing succession of museum exhibitions we have helped mount in connection with Afton Historical Society Press books.

Rena's book received a lot of media attention, some of

it, to her dismay, because she was the Coen brothers' mother. In an article for the *Minneapolis Star Tribune*, Mary Abbe wrote, "Undazzled by the 'Fargo' fame of her two moviemaker sons, the St. Louis Park art historian gets excited about painters instead." More blatant was an interview with Rena that appeared on a local television station. I was with Rena at her home the morning it was filmed, and she asked the television people not to ask her about her sons, and they didn't. That evening when the interview aired, however, Rena's comments were interspersed with clips from *Fargo*.

All of our 1996 books came from the list of books that I was one day going to write myself, but now I was matching these projects with the best qualified authors. For a book about Afton—*Afton Remembered*—I called on longtime resident Ed Robb. Ed is a retired English teacher and writes a local history column for our monthly Afton paper. In 1926 his father purchased one of five houses on Catfish Bar, a long, narrow point of sand that curves out from the Wisconsin shore, across the river from Afton, as a family vacation home. Quoting his brother Wally in *Afton Remembered*, Ed wrote: "If Dad had given each of us a million dollars, it wouldn't have meant as much to us as growing up on the St. Croix."

Afton was settled beginning in the 1840s by New England loggers, followed by German and Swede farmers, and has never been a boom town. Her sawmills were short-lived, and even the local berry business collapsed after World War I. Ed's book was the first history of our little river "city," which today comprises both the former Afton Village, a mere six by ten blocks or four-tenths of a square mile, and Afton Township, a twenty-four square mile area platted in 1858, the year Minnesota achieved statehood. The combined population of the village and the township today hovers around three thousand souls. Afton never lived up to the expectations of its founders, thank goodness, and remains a place apart, an idyllic hamlet where residents treasure its rural character.

The Afton Historical Society, just down the street from us, provided most of the wonderful vintage photographs for *Afton Remembered*. One photo pictures Vice President Walter Mondale and his wife Joan emerging from Afton's Town Hall (an 1868 frame church building now occupied by the Afton Historical Society) after voting on election day in 1976, the year he ran for president. Joan's parents lived in Afton, and it was the Mondales' legal residence. Another Afton Historical Society photo shows famed World War II correspondent Ernie Pyle and his wife Jerry as Ernie leaves for the Pacific, where he will be killed and buried four months later in April 1945. Jerry Pyle died the same year and is buried in Afton, where she grew up, in Evergreen Cemetery.

Afton Remembered was published with financial help from retired General Mills chairman Charlie Bell and his family. Bell began buying property on Valley

Joan and Walter Mondale

Ernie and Jerry Pyle

179

Creek in Afton in 1970 for a family retreat that eventually became the Belwin Outdoor Education Laboratory on more than one thousand acres. Upwards of ten thousand school children each year visit Belwin, which is maintaining the native habitat and preserving eleven at-risk ecosystems, including a native prairie, a beaver work area, a geological drift area, and a woodland pothole, to name a few.

I knew of Charlie Bell because of Belwin, but also because he has always been something of a surrogate father to Duncan MacMillan. Duncan and Bell's son, David Winton Bell, were best friends when they were growing up and went through college together at Brown. On December 26, 1954, six months to the day after he was married, Marine Lieutenant David Bell crashed in the fog in a fighter jet in the Sea of Japan. His pregnant wife, Jo, was on her way to Japan when the accident happened and was met at the plane with the news that David had been lost. Part of the Bell family support for *Afton Remembere*d came from the David Winton Bell Foundation, which his parents established following his death.

Our 1996 list also included *Minnesota Architect: The Life and Work of Clarence H. Johnston* by architectural historian Paul Clifford Larson. Though lesser known than his boyhood friend and lifetime buddy Cass Gilbert, Johnston was Minnesota's most prolific architect. While Gilbert moved on to New York and national fame, Johnston stayed home to become the most sought-after architect for two generations of St. Paul's upper classes. For thirty years, beginning in 1901, he also served as Minnesota State Architect, designing virtually all the buildings on thirty-five state-owned sites and campuses, including the University of Minnesota.

In the 1980s, when I was compiling the White Bear Yacht Club's centennial history, I had become acquainted with Jim Johnston, Jr., Clarence Johnston's grandson. Jim, Jr. was the son of Harrison R. (Jimmy) Johnston, Sr., the yacht club's celebrity golfer. Jim, Sr. won the Minnesota Amateur Championship seven times in a row, 1921 through 1927. In 1929, when he won the National Amateur championship at Pebble Beach, Jim, Sr. returned home to a ticker-tape parade in downtown St. Paul. Amateur golf was at its peak and the title was the foremost honor in American amateur sports.

Clarence H. Johnston

Jim, Jr. provided information about his father and photographs for the White Bear book, and I learned that Jim, Sr.'s father was Clarence Johnston—the single most important figure in the history of Minnesota architecture. This was truly a talented family! In addition to state hospitals and public buildings, Johnston designed dozens of fine houses on Summit Avenue in St. Paul, several of them for White Bear Yacht Club members. There hadn't been a book about Johnston, but he certainly deserved one. I added *The Life and Work of Clarence H. Johnston* to my list of books that needed to be written.

While working with Duncan MacMillan on the *MacGhillemhaoil* volumes, I reconnected with Jim Johnston, Jr. Jim sometimes phoned when I was working with Duncan in his office. Their families were longtime friends; Jim, Sr. had played golf with Duncan's father, John H. MacMillan, Jr., at the Woodhill Country Club in Wayzata. Duncan liked the idea of a book about Clarence Johnston when I mentioned it to him, and Jim, Jr. and his family agreed to fund the research and writing.

We hired architectural historian Paul Larson to provide the manuscript and compile the photographs for *Minnesota Architect: The Life and Work of Clarence H. Johnston.*

Larson was working as director of the Gardner Museum of Architecture and Design in Quincy, Illinois, when I called to ask him if he would be interested in the Johnston project. I had some of Paul's earlier books in my library and was particularly impressed with his book about the work of Boston architect Henry Hobson Richardson and his followers, *The Spirit of H. H. Richardson on the Midland Prairies.* Richardson was the first American architect to give his name to a style—the Richardsonian Romanesque. Paul Larson is a meticulous historian, I've never known better, and he told me, yes, he would write the Johnston book. Exceeding my expectations, he produced the definitive monograph on Clarence Johnston's career, a beautiful book, designed by Barb Arney, that details every known Johnston building.

By the time we sent *Minnesota Architect* to the printer, Jim Johnston, Jr. was dying of lung cancer. We worried he wouldn't live to see it published, but I think this book probably added months to his life. He was the guest of honor at the publication party at the Minnesota Club in St. Paul (which had been designed by his grandfather). Jim's sister and brother-in-law, Janette and John Burton, hosted this very swanky party, and Jim held court at one end of the room in a wing chair, greeting the many friends who came to see him. He was noticeably short of breath that evening, and he died a few weeks later, just before Christmas.

Minnesota Architect: The Life and Work of Clarence H. Johnston won three prestigious awards: a 1997 Minnesota Book Award, the 1997 Midwest Independent Publishers Award in the architecture category, and brand new that year, the 1997 David Stanley Gebhard Award for best architecture book.

Paul Larson moved to St. Paul to write full time and has become Afton's most prolific author. His second book for Afton, in 1997, was *Icy Pleasures: Minnesota Celebrates Winter*, which explores the many ways in which Minnesotans have embraced the state's Siberian reputation with winter carnivals and cold weather sports. *Icy Pleasures* won both a Minnesota Book Award and a Midwest Independent Publishers Award. To boot, Grand Casino, which operates gambling casinos in Hinckley and Mille Lacs, Minnesota, purchased one thousand copies of *Icy Pleasures* to give as gifts to its special gold card members. This purchase remains our largest single order from an individual customer (not a wholesaler or bookstore).

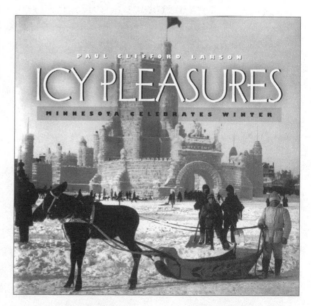

In 1998 Larson followed up *Icy Pleasures* with an equally popular summer book, *A Place at the Lake*, a pictorial account of the summer houses that have proliferated along Minnesota's lakeshores—the humble and the high-style, the nests of logs and the summer palaces. We were both surprised and thrilled when *A Place at the Lake* won a first-place award in a national competition, from Independent Publishers Magazine! We were really moving out.

Some people know us best for our holiday book series, which we began in 1996. The idea was that we would ask a prominent Minnesota writer to write a brief memoir for us each year, something on the order of Truman Capote's *One Christmas*. It was already summer when I thought of this, and too late to commission a book for that year, so instead we reprinted an article that had appeared in *Minnesota History* magazine in 1935. Written by Bertha Heilbron, "Christmas and New Year's on the Minnesota Frontier" (we also used the title of the article for our book) was based on pioneer diaries, beginning in 1827 on Christmas Day, when Indian Agent Major Lawrence Taliaferro at Fort Snelling wrote in his diary:

"Indians both men & women called at 11 oclk . . . in considerable numbers to see & shake hands & express the feelings of the day—which they appear to have taken up within the last Eight years from the Whites. The feelings of their hearts were expressed before I was aware by a few *Yellow Kisses—& amusing Scene*." In 1836, by now heartily tired of the yuletide attentions of the Indian women, Taliaferro complained: "had of course to undergo various salutations on the cheek from many & old as well as young women—a custom derived from our Canadian population— not a very agreeable one."

Christmas & New Year's on the Minnesota Frontier appeared in our first-ever catalog that season, along with the eight other Afton titles we had in print. We printed 1,500 first edition copies of this small book (9" x 6", 64 pages) and still have a few left.

Our next year's holiday book was an unabashed success. Our first printing of 4,000 copies of Bill Holm's *Faces of Christmas Past* sold out in less than four weeks in October, and we published another 4,000 copies in time for Christmas. This book got exceptionally good reviews and publicity. *Minnesota Monthly* printed an excerpt from *Faces* (and paid us for the privilege of doing so!). In a review in *Mpls/St. Paul* magazine, Bill Swanson wrote: "Minnesota's finest prose stylist, tiny Minneota's big Bill Holm, happily (for us) returns to print with this slight, elegant meditation on Yuletide on the prairie."

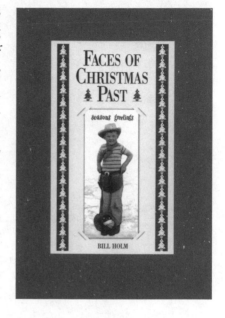

Faces of Christmas Past deserved every praise it received. It's an exceptional memoir that speaks with wit and grace to the perils of Christmas and self-imposed burdens of ritual duty (like the newsy Christmas xerox). It is also the first book in which Bill writes about his mother, Jonina Sigurborg Josephson Holm ("Jona"). Raised without money in an Icelandic immigrant farm family, Jona longed for education, travel, adventure, the Big World. Instead she married her high school sweetheart, Big Bill Holm, and moved to another immigrant farm a few miles from her parents—no college, no career, no New York.

"She didn't whine," Bill wrote. "If luck and circumstance thwarted her longing for beauty, elegance, an exciting life, she [invented] her own version of them wherever she was. . . . She crocheted, she knitted, she embroidered, she painted figurines and wooden plates and breadboards . . . she glued beads and gewgaws on any recyclable object,

Jon Hassler and Bill Holm, with bookseller Anita Zager, signing books in Duluth, 1998

however unlikely . . . Her house became the gallery for her projects and at Christmas, her favorite season, the show doubled or tripled in size to overwhelm the cramped little farmstead. . . . What she made was not 'kitsch'; kitsch implies a consciousness of fashionable taste satirically undermined. Jona invented beauty—as she understood it."

Our holiday book series was seeming like a good idea, and with our 1998 holiday book we wandered accidentally, and providentially, into fiction. I had gotten up the courage to ask Jon Hassler, my literary hero, for a Christmas memoir, and he had agreed to write one. Then, months later, with the due date for his manuscript approaching, Jon got in touch with me to say that his memoir had turned into a short story, was that OK? I didn't have to give this much thought. Jon hadn't written a short story in twenty years. My answer was a resounding "Yes!"

A few weeks later I met Jon for lunch at the Chicago Deli in Minneapolis, where he gave me the manuscript for *Underground Christmas*. Until then we hadn't talked about money. Now I told him that our usual advance for our holiday books was $1,000 against royalties. Jon said that was fine. It wasn't until the next year, when I was negotiating with him for a book of his short stories, that Jon mentioned that his last advance from Ballantine had been $150,000.

My husband, Charlie, did the cover painting for

Underground Christmas, a pastel of the old church at St. John's University in Collegeville, where Jon taught Minnesota Authors and Creative Writing for seventeen years. *Underground Christmas* is about a man named Jay who has come rather late to his midlife crisis. Nearing fifty, Jay finds himself dislocated by a divorce (from a lesbian wife) and by his only child's attempted suicide. Seeking stability, he has taken a temporary teaching position at his alma mater, St. Andrew's College (which sounds suspiciously like St. John's). Part One of this three-part story opens in the school's potting shed, which in earlier days had been a root cellar, where Jay and his close friend Charlie, who is on the brink of ordination to the priesthood, are part of a small Christmas Eve gathering.

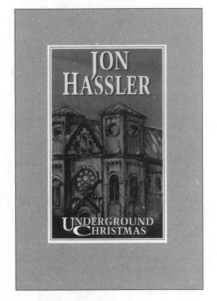

Mpls/St. Paul magazine published the concluding Part Three to *Underground Christmas* in its December issue that year. The setting is Rookery State Hospital, where Jay pays a Christmas visit to his son Bob, a recovering alcoholic. In this final, poignant episode, it becomes apparent that if Jay is going to recover his equilibrium, Bob will be a factor in his recovery. *Underground Christmas* is not your usual holiday story. It is classic Hassler, and we knew we had a winner. We ordered 8,000 copies and sold almost all of them that first season.

Jon then asked me if we would be interested in publishing some of his early short stories (written before Atheneum took a chance on an unknown author and published his first novel, *Staggerford*). The resulting book was *Keepsakes & Other Stories* (1998). Fans lined up out the doors at the many book signings we scheduled throughout the state. We had planned to print 5,000 hardcover copies, but at the last minute, with prepublication orders pouring in, we upped our print run to 7,000 books. Even so, demand for Jon's short stories so out-stripped our expectations that we ordered 10,000 softcover copies of *Keepsakes* before Christmas.

Not only were we publishing Jon Hassler in the late 1990s, we were also involved in the production of our first television documentary, based on our book *Death of the Dream* by St. Paul photographer and essayist Bill Gabler. Bill had come to see me in 1996 with a huge book he had compiled of his photographs of abandoned farmhouses and accompanying text. It was truly an astounding work. Gabler is an amateur geologist who had become aware of the widespread deterioration of nineteenth-century farmhouses while driving throughout Minnesota and neighboring states to study rocks and land forms.

"It seemed to me that something wonderful had passed away, and nothing was coming in its place," he told me. "The old farmhouses were doomed, there was no way to save them, but their great homeliness and variety could be recorded in photographs." To create a visual record of early farm life in Minnesota, Gabler had ended up driving sixty thousand miles of rural roads and taking five thousand photographs. Many of the houses he documented have since disappeared.

I couldn't guess how much of a market we would have for this book, but the black-and-white photographs were stunning, and I knew the project was too good to turn away. Barb Arney designed *Death of the Dream*, which we published in hardcover with the subtitle *Classic Minnesota Farmhouses*. It's a remarkably beautiful and haunting book, 10" x 11" (much smaller than the one Bill had put together by hand), 128 pages, with more than seventy tritone plates. Gabler made a substantial monetary gift to the Afton Historical Society Press that covered some of our printing costs and enabled us to price his book at just $35.

In our small catalog that year, we called *Death of the Dream* "A New Minnesota Classic!" We did not know how right we were! *Death of the Dream* would turn out to be our first really *HUGE* success.

The Afton Press was growing and our staff increasing. We were still operating out of one room in the Afton Market Square Building when Bill Gabler first came to see me, but in March 1997 we moved down the street to three rooms in an addition to the old Afton bank building. This is really terrific space, designed by Stillwater architect Mike McGuire in the tradition of Frank Lloyd Wright with lots of glass and timbers. My spacious second-floor office looks out through floor-to-ceiling windows on the slow-flowing St. Croix River.

Our small office was managed by Barb Arney's daughter, Michelle Nelson (until the next year when she gave birth to her own daughter.) My daughter Mary Sue helped with publicity and just about everything. My next-door neighbor Adrien Porter worked part-time as our

Bill Gabler photos from Death of the Dream

bookkeeper. Adrien and her husband Bob Porter have always been perfect and very helpful neighbors, and Adrien was wonderful to work with. She used a computer to keep accounts, not a pencil as I had, and by now we had our own checking account. We even had a Visa and MasterCard account to accommodate charge customers.

We also now had a marketing director, Paul Druckman, who was changing forever the destiny of this small press. Paul grew up in Brooklyn (and never outgrew his accent) and has more energy and creative ideas than any three people I know, maybe six. I had met Paul in October 1996 at a Minnesota Library Association conference in St. Cloud. Paul was president of the Midwest Independent Publishers Association and was exhibiting MIPA members' books across the aisle from where Mary Sue and I had a table with our six or seven Afton titles.

One of our goals when Paul began working with us was to establish a relationship with local public television station KTCA-TV to produce documentaries based on our books. KTCA had produced some wonderful documentaries based on regional history, films like *Dakota Exile* and *Lost Twin Cities*, and it seemed to us that our books would make similarly excellent films. So Paul made an appointment and went downtown with an armful of our books to call on KTCA.

That meeting would, in three years time, lead to a blockbuster film, but the going was slow at first. KTCA was interested all right. Paul came back and told me that the talk had been about not just one documentary with Afton, but maybe a series of them. Over the next twelve months, however, the station went through some changes, including a new president, and it was a full year before we got back to discussing the details of our first joint project. The subject had not even been identified, but *Seth Eastman: A Portfolio of*

North American Indians and *Minnesota Architect: The Life and Work of Clarence H. Johnston* had been singled out as strong contenders. This year-long delay turned out to be lucky happenstance.

Afton Press had led off its spring season in 1997 with Bill Gabler's *Death of the Dream*, and the book was attracting a lot of attention. It was a story that struck a chord in many, many people who had grown up on farms or had relatives on them. KTCA liked it too and decided that this was the story the station wanted to produce. Afton agreed with this choice, and KTCA retained six-time Emmy-award winning director and independent film producer John Whitehead to write the script and direct *Death of the Dream: Farmhouses in the Heartland*. (The subtitle was changed from *Classic Minnesota Farmhouses* because we all felt that this film would have a wide audience across the country.)

Fred de Sam Lazaro, KTCA's long-time correspondent for *The NewsHour* with Jim Lehrer was named executive producer for the *Death of the Dream* film. John Whitehead would also serve as co-producer with KTCA's Michael Trosman. The KTCA people prepared a story outline and preliminary budget, and we were in the movie business. Well, almost. There was still the small matter of money. The KTCA budget specified $276,000, which we planned to raise jointly. As it turned out, we didn't have to.

John Whitehead shot some initial footage and KTCA hosted an early evening gathering for those of us involved in this project. Besides John Whitehead and Fred de Sam Lazaro, the KTCA people included President Jim Pagliarini and Vice President Bill Hanley. Duncan and his wife, Nivin, joined Paul Druckman and me from Afton Press. Duncan and Nivin MacMillan were still almost newlyweds, having been married in September 1996. We all liked Whitehead's preliminary footage, no question, and Nivin, who is relatively new to the Midwest, after living most of her life in the East, was especially enthusiastic. John Whitehead is an incredible talent, and it was already obvious from the brief film clips he showed us, and his descriptions of what he intended to do, that he was putting his heart and soul into this film.

Duncan called me the next morning at my office. "Do you want me to do this?" he asked. He was asking me if I wanted him to fund the *Death of the Dream* documentary. This took me by surprise, as we had anticipated having to raise the money elsewhere, but I was delighted. "That would be wonderful," I replied.

"Tell them that we'll give them $200,000," Duncan told me. So I went to KTCA with this figure, and *Death of the Dream* was made for that $200,000, not a penny more. Filming was

spread out over a twelve-month period to take advantage of all four seasons on the farm, and we all—Duncan, Paul, Charlie, and I—got to play like movie people one day, filming on location at the historic Oliver Kelley farm, which is operated by the Minnesota Historical Society in Anoka, Minnesota. Duncan makes a cameo appearance in *Death of the Dream*. You'll see him hammering nails into a piece of lumber, then, later, leading a team of workhorses back to the barn.

On November 15, 1999, Afton Press sponsored an advance screening of *Death of the Dream* for the media and special friends and par-

Duncan MacMillan in outtake from
Death of the Dream

On location, Paul, me, Duncan, and Charlie

ticipants in the film at the Minnesota History Center in St. Paul. Paul Druckman dreamed up and orchestrated this affair, and it was a hugely successful party, with wonderful food, as are all of the press events and publication parties Paul arranges for Afton. Director John Haworth of the Smithsonian's National Museum of the American Indian in New York flew in (and stayed to discuss our next documentary, about Seth Eastman and his portfolio of paintings of Native Americans). *Publishers Weekly*, the national trade magazine for the book industry, was represented by Matt Hurley (who would later entertain us and show us the ropes at the London Book Fair). One direct and immediate result of this screening was a great deal of media coverage for *Death of the Dream* that helped boost broadcast ratings.

Going beyond the book that inspired it, the *Death of the Dream* film documents the dignity of a vanishing lifestyle. Told by historians, farm experts, and most importantly, the people who lived "The Dream" of life on the farm, it charts the impact that changing economics have had on the lives of Midwestern farm families. Narrated by Linda Kelsey (of *The Lou Grant Show*), the film features poets Robert Bly and Leo Dangel, writers Bill Holm and Paul Gruchow, with original music by Steve Heitzeg. To coincide with the premier of the public television documentary, we reprinted *Death of the Dream* in softcover. Afton is also the distributor for the home video and music CD versions of *Death of the Dream*.

KTCA aired *Death of the Dream* during prime time both the day before and the day after Thanksgiving. It proved so popular that the station subsequently broadcast it three times during December pledge week. KTCA estimated that by the end of the year it had been seen by more than 200,000 families in the Twin Cities area. Then it went national! By summer 2000, *Death of the Dream* was airing on public television stations throughout the country. We were receiving orders for the video, the book, and the CD from California and Florida and Maine and Connecticut, actually thirty-eight states at last count.

The PBS website at www.pbs.org posted fifty pages about *Death of the Dream*. Our AHSP website at www.afton-press.com has streaming video from the documentary and a photo gallery from the book. My son Chuck Johnston created and maintains our Afton website. He is also the wizard who keeps all of our computer equipment up and running.

10

New York, New York!

ON ONE OF THE BEST DAYS in summer, 1998, we launched two new books with a yachting excursion on Lake Minnetonka: *A Place at the Lake* by Paul Larson and *MacMillan: The American Grain Family* by Duncan MacMillan. This was a media event, planned and coordinated by Paul Druckman, for fifty print, radio, and television newspeople, all of whom looked to be having a grand time. I know I did. I had bought a new dress for this outing—my family said it looked "Egyptian"—and a "movie star" hat, a big, brown, floppy, broad-brimmed affair. Paul Larson came dressed in a flowered print shirt that had vacation written all over it.

Both *A Place at the Lake* and *MacMillan* have obvious Lake Minnetonka connections. *A Place at the Lake*, Larson's opus on summer homes, opens on Minnetonka, which was once the greatest tourist draw in the state. By the late nineteenth century, Lake Minnetonka's jagged shoreline (variously estimated at two to three hundred miles) and the embankments above boasted five hundred seasonal dwellings and a dozen fine hotels.

In the present day, quoting Larson (who narrated a tour of the homes we were seeing that day), "Architects . . . have made [Lake Minnetonka] a showplace of modernest versions of life in nature, from woodsy [Frank Lloyd Wright-like] retreats to vast walls of glass."

Duncan's book, *MacMillan*, is also set partially on Lake Minnetonka. His family has lived and prospered there for three generations. After renting a cottage on Minnetonka for two seasons, Duncan's grandfather, John H. MacMillan, Sr., began building a year-round home in 1930 on eighty acres that would become the family compound. According to the *Minnetonka Herald*, John, Sr.'s residence was second in size only to the sixty-room edifice being put up at Gray's Bay by Wayzata Mayor Rufus R. Rand—the chateau-like structure that now houses Cargill's world headquarters.

Duncan MacMillan with his sister Marnie

Duncan grew up and learned to sail on Lake Minnetonka. "Sailing was an important part of my life all through the 1940s and my college years," he wrote in *MacMillan*. "My father started us [Duncan, his brother Hugh, and sister Marnie] off early with an X boat and sailing lessons at the Minnetonka Yacht Club. . . . I had a hot hand and won a lot of silver." On the day of our Afton excursion, Duncan and his wife Nivin motored over in a small launch from the Wayzata side of Lake Minnetonka to meet us at the dock in Excelsior. The rest of us had arrived by car or the bus Paul Druckman had chartered for media people.

It was a *perfect* summer day, sunny and warm, but not

too warm, just right. The yacht was splendid; the scenery, breathtaking; and the food, terrific. Duncan's birthday was coming up, so for dessert we included a cake that said "MacMillan." Both authors discussed their books, and our audience was truly "captive," out there in a boat on the lake.

This one media event generated tons of publicity for both books. Local Twin Cities television station KARE ran footage from the launch party on its five o'clock evening news program, and WCCO-TV aired reporter Esme Murphy's interview from the event a few days later. The Sunday *Minneapolis Star Tribune* featured *MacMillan* on a front section page, and *Mpls/St. Paul* and *Architecture Minnesota* magazines printed excerpts from *A Place at the Lake*. Paul Larson appeared on numerous television shows, Duncan MacMillan was a guest on radio broadcasts, and dozens of other magazines and newspapers also touted these two books.

Duncan and Nivin MacMillan on Lake Minnetonka

Publicity is all-important to launching a new book or how else will people know about it, become excited about it, and want to purchase it? At Afton we go all out to put on the best publication party/media events possible. We first of all dream up a very attractive event that we think will appeal to reporters. Who could resist an afternoon on a great boat with great food on Lake Minnetonka, for example? Then we send out our invitations early, usually three weeks or more in advance. We also place follow-up telephone calls to editors and reporters, urging them to join us, telling them what they're going to miss by not being on hand. Even when the people we're reaching can't attend, these personal phone calls help build and nourish good relationships with the media. We also maintain a database of hundreds of media contacts to whom we send review copies of our books.

Most of our books appeal to fairly wide audiences, but we also publish an occasional book of exceptional quality intended mainly for scholars and collectors. Such a book, one of our all-time proudest publishing accomplishments, is *Peoples of the Twilight: European Views of Native Minnesota, 1823-1865* by Christian Feest and Sylvia Kasprycki, which also came out in 1998. Christian had suggested this book to me after annotating the Plates for *Seth Eastman: A Portfolio of North American Indians*. He explained to me that a great deal of ethnic material had been brought back to Europe by early

visitors to our part of the world and was now in European—particularly German and Austrian—museums.

Breaking new ground, *Peoples of the Twilight* brought together forty-two little known drawings by European artists (Johann Baptist Wengler, Fredrika Bremer, Adolph Hoeffler, and Franz Hölzlhuber), a daguerreotype, and photographs of forty artifacts collected by European travelers (including Giocomo Costantino Beltrami, Albert-Alexandre de Pourtalès, and Vojta Náprstek) to illustrate aspects of the lifeways of the Dakota, Ojibwe, and Winnebago peoples prior to the Indian Wars of 1862. The artifacts include Dakota dolls, cradle boards, an umbilical cord amulet, a medicine bag, a wooden "courting" flute, gunstock clubs, a pipe tomahawk, a wood-

A Dakota cradle board, pre-1830

en dance mirror, and several catlinite pipes. The accompa-

nying text is based on the written accounts of better and lesser known European observers (Frederick Marryat, Joseph N.
Nicollet, Francesco Arese, F. V. Lamare-Picquot, Moritz Wagner
and Karl Scherzer, Aleksandr B. Lakier, Father Franz Pierz, and
others).

We usually print five to ten thousand copies of a new
book, but because of the specialized nature of *Peoples*, we
printed only 900 trade edition copies plus 100 signed and
numbered limited edition copies. The latter were handbound at the Campbell-Logan Bindery in Minneapolis in
handmade English marbled paper-covered boards with
goatskin spines and fore-edges. The slipcase is covered in a
gorgeous, red Japanese silk. I've never seen a more beautiful
book. Christian Feest helped market this book by advertising it in the *European Review of Native American Studies*,
which he edits and publishes in Frankfurt, Germany.

From early on we have had occasional help from free-
lance editors, one of whom, Sally Rubinstein, works full-
time for the Minnesota Historical Society Press, where she is
the resident expert on Native American subjects. Sally edited our two Eastman books in 1995, *Seth Eastman: A Portfolio
of North American Indians* and *Dahcotah; or, Life and Legends of
the Sioux*. She also edited all three of Paul Larson's books—
Minnesota Architect: The Life and Work of Clarence H. Johnston,
Icy Pleasures: Minnesota Celebrates Winter, and *A Place at the
Lake*—as well as Bill Gabler's *Death of the Dream*.

One day Sally and I were having lunch at Tulips, a
superb little French restaurant on Selby Avenue in St. Paul,
talking books, when she asked me if I had ever read any of
Mabel Seeley's books. No, I hadn't, I said. I wasn't familiar
with her work.

Sally went on to tell me that Mabel Seeley was a
Minnesota author who had written mysteries set in her

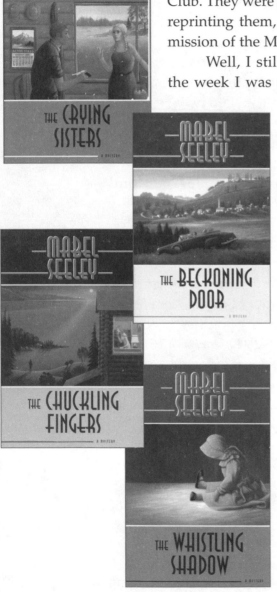

home state beginning in the late 1930s up into the early 1950s. Her books were published by Doubleday in New York and distributed by the prestigious Crime Club. They were great reads, and somebody should be reprinting them, Sally said, but they fell outside the mission of the Minnesota Historical Society Press.

Well, I still liked a good mystery, and within the week I was able to pick up a couple of Mabel's books, *The Beckoning Door* and *The Chuckling Fingers,* at local second-hand bookstores. *The Beckoning Door,* which I read first, is about a young woman, Cathy Kingman, who resents the circumstances that have kept her in the stifling mid-Minnesota resort community of Long Meadow. When her rich cousin Sylvia is found dead, Cathy becomes suspect and must find the real murderer or become the next victim! I read this story, cover to cover, in one afternoon; I couldn't put it down. *The Chuckling Fingers,* which I liked even better, was promoted as *the* mystery of the year in 1940, and takes place at a lumberman's estate on Lake Superior, north of Grand Marais.

The Afton Press had never intended to publish fiction, but it seemed to me that, given these books' Minnesota settings, our particular mission should be stretched

200

to embrace this type of classic mystery story. This was also right about the time that Jon Hassler told me that his memoir had turned into a short story. So we rewrote our mission statement.

Our original mission statement, written when we founded Afton in 1993, began: "The Afton Historical Society Press publishes books that adhere to high standards of scholarship, design, and production on Minnesota subjects." After "high standards of scholarship," we inserted "literary value." (In our current mission statement, we have dropped the word "Minnesota" in favor of "regional.")

We needed to obtain the rights to reprint these books, so we tracked down Mabel Seeley's son, Greg Seeley, in New Jersey. Greg told us that Doubleday in New York still owned the rights to his mother's mystery novels. When we contacted Doubleday, the people there were glad to learn of our interest and, for a total price of $2,000, sold us the rights to reprint 4,000 copies each of four of Mabel Seeley's mysteries. We published *The Beckoning Door* and *The Chuckling Fingers* in 1998, The *Whistling Shadow* in 1999, and *The Crying Sisters* in 2000.

Mystery author Mabel Seeley

Once we had the first two Seeley books in print, we heard from Mabel's brother, Franklin Hodnefield, who was in his nineties and lived in a St. Paul suburb. Mr. Hodnefield had all seven of his sister's mysteries and allowed us to make copies of those we didn't have. He also loaned us the photograph of Mabel that appears on the back of each of our Afton Press editions. Another relative called from Indiana to say that Mabel had a glass eye, which is why photographs of her show her looking down.

We also heard from Mabel Seeley fan Dennis Crow in Oregon, who offered, at no cost to us, out of the goodness of his heart, to do some biographical research for us on the author. Dennis provided the material that enabled me to write the Publisher's Note about Mabel that appears in our Afton Press edition of *The Whistling Shadow*.

The new cover paintings for all four Afton Press books were created by St. Paul artist Paul S. Kramer, who is himself a Minnesota treasure. Now in his late seventies, Paul still maintains a painting studio on Kellogg Boulevard, across the street from the Minnesota History Center (which includes several of his paintings in its collections). Paul has spent most of his life painting Minnesota landscapes and often peoples them with wonderfully odd-looking figures that bear a resemblance to the strange inhabitants in some of Edward Hopper's paintings.

I've known Paul for a long time. When I was fourteen or fifteen, I applied for a job modeling at the St. Paul School of Art where he was teaching evening classes. The person who took my application over the phone asked me if I did life or costume modeling. Well, I didn't have any costumes, so I said "life." When I heard from the school a few weeks later, the woman on the phone asked me how old I was and if I knew what "life" meant. I hadn't known that "life" meant nude, and she suggested I wear a leotard. For two nights I modeled for figure-drawing classes Paul was teaching.

My dad was out of town that week. When he returned and heard what I was doing, he wasn't happy about it and told me to stop. This was just fine with me. I'd already had enough of standing still for two hours at a stretch for $1.50 an hour. Modeling for Paul's art classes had turned out to be strenuous work and something I've never done again. I do, however, love Paul's paintings of regional subjects and have been lucky enough to acquire several of them over the years.

Barb Arney had been designing most of our beautiful Afton Press books, but after her husband, Dick Arney, died in early 1998, my daughter Mary Sue began doing more of our design work. Barb had designed the first Mabel Seeley book, *The Beckoning Door*, and Mary Sue took over for the next three Seeley titles. Mary Sue also designed Jon Hassler's *Keepsakes & Other Stories* for us in 1998. By this time she had bought a house and was living and singing in Nashville. With today's technology, Mary Sue can do her design work in Nashville and e-mail the page layouts, cover designs, everything, directly to us or to the printer.

We were also busy, very busy, in 1998 with a complex book titled *Ralph Rapson: Sixty Years of Modern Design* that would accompany a joint exhibition of the same name at the Minneapolis Institute of Arts (MIA) and the Frederick R. Weisman Museum of Art at the University of Minnesota. Christopher Monkhouse and Jennifer Olivarez, the curators for the MIA portion of the exhibition, had come to see us early in the year, along with the book's three authors, Rip Rapson, Jane King Hession, and Bruce N. Wright, proposing that we take on this book project. We immediately said yes.

The authors' credentials were impressive. Rip Rapson, Ralph Rapson's son, has a law degree from Columbia and was working as a senior fellow at the University of Minnesota's Design Center for American Urban Landscape. (Since the publication of *Ralph Rapson*, but not because of it, he has gone on to become the president of the McKnight Foundation in Minneapolis, one of this country's largest philanthropic organizations.) Jane King Hession is an architectural historian and was guest curator for the Weisman's portion of the Ralph Rapson exhibition. Bruce Wright is an architect and the editor of *Fabrics and Architecture* magazine.

Ralph Rapson's reputation is monumental. He is the most influential Minnesota architect of the twentieth century. Trained in the late 1930s under Eliel Saarinen at the Cranbrook Academy of Art, he has played a leading role in the development and practice of modern architecture. In postwar Europe, his designs for nine U.S. embassy projects established a new international model for the American embassy abroad. In the Twin Cities, his best-known projects include the landmark Tyrone Guthrie Theater (1963), and Cedar Square West, an innovative urban-renewal project for one of Minneapolis's oldest working-class neighborhoods (1973). Beginning in 1954, Ralph Rapson also headed the University of Minnesota's School of Architecture for thirty years. He transformed the school and also the standing of the design profession within the state.

Ralph Rapson

Ralph Rapson celebrated his eighty-sixth birthday in 2000 and was still keeping regular office hours, on Cedar Avenue in Minneapolis, across the street from his famed Cedar Square West project. (Years ago I saw a scale model of Cedar Square West in one of the Smithsonian museums.) Some of his recent commissions included the South Korean Embassy in Moscow and the Jang-Baek Mountain Resort in China. He was also designing a new conservatory building for the Minnesota Landscape Arboretum in Chanhassen.

Famous for his exquisite architectural renderings, Ralph has lived out his life with what would seem to be a serious handicap for an architect. His lower right arm was amputated at birth. Drawing nevertheless became the method by which he communicated his ideas, and he learned to do so rapidly, fluently, and beautifully. *Ralph Rapson: Sixty Years of Modern Design* contains hundreds of Ralph's architectural drawings, and he also created an architectural time line of significant buildings—his own and those of other architects—that runs through it.

Ralph Rapson signing books at national American Institute of Architects (AIA) convention in Dallas, 1999

The Rapson book project turned out to be more complex than any of us had imagined. All three authors were working on *Rapson* concurrently, writing different chapters (there are twelve in all), and the manuscript wasn't finished in April when we first expected it, and it continued unfinished into the final months of the year. In the meantime, since the exhibition was opening in March 1999, we began editing the chapters that were complete and putting them into page layouts. This is a very difficult way to produce a book, we learned the hard way, and resulted in numerous changes having to be made to both copy and layouts all along the way.

Everyone connected with this project worked heroically on it. This included editor Phil Freshman, a former Minnesota Historical Society Press editor who now has his own free-lance business, and book designer Kristi Anderson of Two Spruce Design in Minneapolis. Sally Rubinstein completed the comprehensive index in what must been record time during the project's final days.

At the same time that they were writing their chapters, the authors also raised $60,000, mostly from the local architectural community, to help with production costs. This enabled us to price this substantial two-color, hardcover book (11" x 11", 256 pages) at just $35. Donors were acknowledged on the copyright page. We also produced 100 handbound copies in silk-covered slipcases. Each limited edition book is numbered and

Friesen's book printing plant in Altona

signed by the authors and contains an original watercolor sketch by Ralph Rapson. (It also occurred to us that these watercolor sketches would themselves make a wonderful book, and we're talking about this with Ralph.)

Ralph Rapson was printed in Canada, in the small town of Altona, Manitoba, by Friesens, a firm we have come to rely on to provide us with high-quality books in a timely fashion. These people are Mennonites with a wonderful work ethic and thoroughly modern and up-to-date printing facilities. Charlie and I have made several trips to Altona to oversee the printing of various books. Friesens puts us up in an apartment across the street from their plant that they keep for visiting publishers.

Prior to the opening of the museum exhibitions at MIA and the Weisman, we organized a well-attended luncheon for local media people at the Rapson-designed Guthrie Theater. We also sent press releases and review copies of *Ralph Rapson* to selected architectural book reviewers throughout the country. *Ralph Rapson: Sixty Years of Modern Design* ended up receiving more publicity, including national and even international attention, than any book we have ever published. The year

Speaking to media people at Guthrie Theater

1999 was off to a terrific start and it would only get better.

We were also laying grand plans to exhibit the MacMillan Collection of Seth Eastman watercolors in New York, something we had set out to accomplish ever since Duncan purchased the paintings. This fit our mission of extending the reach of our publishing program with museum exhibitions and public television documentaries. In July, Duncan and Nivin MacMillan, Paul Druckman, and I flew to New York to meet with Director John Haworth and members of his staff at the George Gustav Heye Center of the Smithsonian's National Museum of the American Indian (NMAI). This trip changed my life.

For the past several years I had been pretty confident that I would never fly again. The last time I had flown had been six years earlier when I went to Florida to care for my mother. Then Jane had died the day after I returned home. Charlie had quit flying even before that, and I had convinced myself that I was afraid to fly and that I didn't have to, for any reason.

In New York

Paul Druckman changed my mind. He put together a trip I couldn't resist. We needed to meet with the Smithsonian people and I should be there, he said. I was the publisher and director of the press. Until now, Paul had been traveling back and forth to New York by himself, making friends with John Haworth and others at NMAI, laying the groundwork for our collaboration. This time, we'd make a party out of it, six of us, he said, Duncan and Nivin MacMillan, Paul and his wife, Jean Hardginski, and Charlie and me. Outside of our Smithsonian meetings, we could have some fun and act like tourists for a couple of days.

Charlie decided to wait for me at home, but Jean joined us, and we *did* have fun. The George Gustav Heye Center is located in the marble-pillared U.S. Custom House designed by Cass Gilbert at Bowling Green in Manhattan. It is an exceptional museum with extraordinary collections that are reason enough for a trip to New York.

George Gustav Heye was a wealthy and insatiable turn-of-the-century collector who in 1916 founded the Museum of the American Indian–Heye Collection to house his personal hoard of four hundred thousand Native American artifacts. Self-indulgent and obsessive, Heye spent sixty-two of his eighty years seeking out and acquiring objects from New World cultures. He bought artifacts at auction, from dealers, from other collectors, and made more than fifty buying trips to Europe. For many years he criss-crossed North America in his chauffeur-driven limousine, buying directly from Indians in their communities. His museum, at Audubon Terrace in Washington Heights in New York City, led eventually to the formation of NMAI, whose holdings today are approximately ten times what Heye turned over in 1916.

Director John Haworth was a warm and cordial host. I liked him immediately, and he has become a good friend. Following our meeting in NMAI's board room to discuss exhibiting the Eastman paintings, he took us to lunch around the corner at historic Fraunces Tavern (where in 1785 George Washington delivered a farewell speech to his troops, and which for the next two years while New York was the capital city, housed the U.S. Departments of Foreign Affairs, Treasury, and War). That evening we celebrated Duncan's birthday with dinner at Picoline, a small, swanky French restaurant, and afterwards rode in the MacMillans' rented limousine to see *Ragtime*, my first Broadway show. On the Fourth of July, before returning home in the afternoon,

The National Museum of the American Indian in New York

Paul and Jean and I took a boat tour around the Statue of Liberty and toured Ellis Island.

This trip really *did* change my life. Having once gotten my wings, I have since learned to love flying. The very next month, in August, I flew to Nashville with Dave and Pat Oleson, my daughter Mary Sue's in-laws, in their compact, six-passenger plane. Mary Sue and her band were performing at the Wild Horse Saloon in downtown Nashville. Mary Sue's husband and partner, David Oleson, plays lead guitar and also does vocals. The Wild Horse is quite the place, absolutely huge, with second and third-level balconies overlooking the dance floor. The stage must be one hundred feet across, maybe more.

With my daughter, Mary Sue, and my son-in-law, David Oleson

Mary Sue and David write most of their own songs, which they also have available on CD. The name of the band is simply "Mary Sue Englund." Watching and applauding them the two nights I was in Nashville with the Olesons was one of the highlights of my year. I was the proudest mother imaginable! Mary Sue also now has a web site at: www.marysueenglund.com

I am also continuing to fly on behalf of the Afton Press. After coming home from Nashville, in September, Paul Druckman and I flew to Washington, D.C., at the invitation of John Haworth to attend the ground-breaking for the Smithsonian's new National Museum of the American Indian on the Mall (just below the Capitol and opposite the East Wing of the National Gallery of Art).

In November, following what I called the "world premier" of our *Death of the Dream* documentary at the Minnesota History Center, Paul and I flew to New Jersey and New York to meet with one of our wholesalers, Baker & Taylor in New Jersey, and *Publishers Weekly* and Barnes & Noble people in New York. This time we were lucky enough to be in New York at the same time that Jon and Gretchen Hassler were calling on his New York publishers with his next novel, *Agatha at Eighty.* Jon had told us that they would be celebrating Gretchen's birthday in New York and suggested we catch up with them. The four of us had dinner at a toney Italian restaurant, and Paul arranged for tickets for us to see *Cats.*

I was liking traveling more all the time, and I was enjoying meeting the people we were doing business with. Baker & Taylor distributes Afton books to booksellers and libraries, both nationally and internationally. *Publishers Weekly*, particularly in the person of Matt Hurley, has been especially helpful to Afton Press in a number of instances and also publishes reviews of our books. At Barnes & Noble headquarters, we arranged for national distribution of John Hassler's latest book, *Keepsakes & Other Stories*. While dining with Jon Hassler in New York, we discussed his third book for Afton, *Rufus at the Door & Other Stories.*

In addition to *Ralph Rapson, The Whistling Shadow,* and Jon Hassler's *Keepsakes*, our new books in 1999 included our holiday book, *An Adolescent's Christmas: 1944*, by Carol Bly. Carol is a brilliant thinker of strong convictions, and her book is a serious one, about a wartime Christmas in Duluth.

Young Carol has two weeks home from boarding school in the East. Her mother has been dead two years, and of her three brothers, all in uniform, two are away at war. Her father meets her on the brick train platform but after driving her home is anxious to get back to work. (He owns and manages the Spaulding Hotel.) Carol arranges the crèche and admires the tree all right, but she also spends time at home writing medium bad sonnets and plans to kiss "that boy in someone's rumpus room if he was the same one I thought he was." Underneath all that, she has nightmares about Germans, and genocide.

"What does it mean if a fourteen-year-old member of an affectionate, loyal, and at least 'three-quarters cultured' family has bad dreams about the Gestapo?" Carol writes. "What are our fourteen-year-olds having nightmares about today?" Recalling her own ad-olescent thinking, and think-ing of what teenagers experi-ence now, Carol comes to some astonishing conclusions.

My mother, Betty Condon, with statue of F. Scott Fitzgerald in front of Landmark Center

In September, commenc-ing an exciting and busy fall season, we invited friends and customers to a publication party at the Landmark Center in St. Paul for Jon Hassler (*Keepsakes & Other Stories*) and Carol Bly (*An Adolescent's Christmas*). Three hundred people showed up to help us celebrate. We served cham-pagne and sandwiches and cakes and sold lots of books. My mother was on hand for the party and enjoyed visiting with Jon and Gretchen Hassler. Mom comes to visit for a couple weeks each fall for her birthday on September 24 (which is also the birthday of Scott Fitzgerald, who was born in St. Paul in 1896).

Jon Hassler signing books at Afton Press booth at UMBA

The next day we had the best-looking booth at the Upper Midwest Booksellers Association (UMBA) trade show in St. Paul. (We design our own booths, and Afton Press always has the best one at every trade show.) The UMBA exhibition was a two-day event that took place on a Saturday and Sunday at the St. Paul Civic Center, and Afton Press had several authors there, signing books for booksellers. Saturday evening, following the show, we walked across Rice Park to the St. Paul Hotel for an authors' dinner Afton hosted for Jon and Gretchen Hassler, Bill Holm, Carol Bly, and Tony Andersen. Our guests also included Mary Ann Grossmann from the *St. Paul Pioneer Press*, Matt Hurley from *Publishers Weekly*, and WCCO-TV personality Bill Carlson and his wife Nancy Nelson. I love dropping all these names!

The UMBA show was followed by the annual Minnesota Library Association (MLA) conference in Duluth

(MLA moves to various locations each year), and we took our books up there. Then we took books to the annual Wisconsin Library Association (WLA) conference in La Crosse. We also sponsored several impressive author events.

Now that we were publishing the big three of Minnesota literature (Bill Holm, Jon Hassler, and Carol Bly), we organized three very special events. We had all three authors on the same stage for programs at Southwest State University at Marshall, Minnesota (where Bill Holm teaches), Gustavus Adolphus College in St. Peter, Minnesota, and the downtown Minneapolis Public Library. These were incredibly energizing literary evenings, with Bill reading from *Faces of Christmas Past*, Jon from *Keepsakes & Other Stories*, and Carol from *An Adolescent's Christmas*. Bill finished off each program with a classical piano piece. He also sometimes plays terrific ragtime at our events.

By December, besides keeping up with all the book and video orders pouring in, we were readying two spring 2000 titles for the printer: *Small Town Minnesota: A to Z* by photojournalist Tony Andersen and *Rufus at the Door & Other Stories* by Jon Hassler. Paul Kramer was at work on the cover painting for our fourth Mabel Seeley mystery, *The Crying Sisters*. We were also negotiating to buy the building in Afton in which we

Bill Holm, Carol Bly, and Jon Hassler in Marshall, Minnesota

had been renting office space. I had the best office in town, with its glorious view of the St. Croix River, and didn't want to chance losing it. We also had run out of office space to support our growing activities. As good as this all sounds, however, and it was in terms of the Afton Press, this month had its difficult days for me personally.

On December 15, I was on the phone with attorney Charlie Carpenter, who was handling the purchase of our building, when my assistant, Sue Andraschko, put a note on my desk. Mark Gherty was on his way over to take me to lunch. I knew what it was about. I had known all along that the damages portion of our civil trial against James Neumann was taking place that morning in a St. Croix County Courtroom.

In June 1997, when twelve jurors found that Neumann had murdered our daughter Jane, we had not, as is usual in a civil case, pursued the subsequent damages portion of the trial. We weren't interested in money, only in shedding light on Jane's death. Because the damages phase had not taken place, however, Neumann found that he could not appeal the verdict to a higher court. So in December 1999 it was Neumann who had brought the action to determine damages that was being heard that day. He had opted not to pay to have jurors, so the case was being decided by Judge Eric Lundell, who had heard the civil case.

It was either very good or very bad news that would bring Mark to my office, and he arrived within minutes of his phone call. We decided to go across the street to the Afton House for a sandwich, and Mark took my arm as we were crossing the street. "Pat," he said, "Judge Lundell ordered Neumann to pay $400,000 in compensatory damages and $5 million in punitive damages."

I went weak in the knees. I hadn't ever thought about massive damages. Mark had mentioned something to me about several hundred thousand dollars in compensatory damages. The reason I hadn't gone to the courtroom that day was that a psychologist was to testify about Jane's pain and suffering from the time she entered her home until she died. I had talked to Mark a week earlier about my reluctance to hear this, and he had told me not to worry, that the judge would understand why I wasn't there. It turned out that Neumann himself "appeared" by telephone, and the only people in the courtroom besides Neumann's attorney were Mark Gherty, Judge Lundell, the court reporter, and AP reporter Chuck Rupnow from the Eau Claire *Leader-Telegram*. Chuck has followed Jane's case since she died and has done an excellent job of reporting about it.

I asked Mark at lunch if he thought I should notify any local media and ended up deciding to call Lorraine Rowe and Robb Leer at KSTP-TV and Esme Murphy at WCCO-TV. I wasn't sure if they would be interested, but these reporters had been extremely supportive and given the case extraordinary coverage. It turned out that the amount of the settlement was one of the largest in a wrongful death case in recent memory. Both television stations hurried a cameraman and reporter to my office to interview me. Both carried the story that night on their evening news programs, along with a lot of earlier footage including some home video of Jane, film from the trial, and family photographs.

Jane's son, Jonny, will be the beneficiary of this settlement money, should all or any part of it eventually be collected from his father. (Charlie and I had filed our wrongful death suit in St. Croix County on behalf of Jonny.) For my part, I am just grateful that this large settlement once again put Jane's death in the news. I don't worry that Jim Neumann will one day be arrested and tried and convicted for her murder. He will be.

11

The Year of the Dragon

CHARLIE AND I watched the spectacular New Year's Day celebrations ringing in the New Millennium around the world on television from our sick bed that day. Mary Sue had come home for Christmas, while her husband David traveled halfway around the world to entertain troops in Bosnia over the holidays, and all three of us—Charlie, Mary Sue, and I—had come down with the flu. Charlie and I had gone to the trouble of having flu shots a few weeks earlier, but they hadn't helped. We were really sick, flat out in bed and aching all over. After about seven days of this, I was becoming depressed and went to see our family doctor, Dr. Dick Powell (who is also a good friend and Charlie's fishing buddy).

"This isn't like me," I told him. "I don't even want to go to work." Dick sympathized with me but said that he couldn't give me anything that would perk me up immediately and that he didn't think I was clinically depressed. Just getting out of bed and going to his office had some beneficial effect. I was no doubt on the mend anyway, and within days I was back to work and happy to be there. From that low point, the new Chinese Year of the Dragon was all uphill.

In February Paul Druckman and I flew to Washington, D.C. to meet with John Haworth and John's boss, Richard

Rick West in Native dress for NMAI gala

With John Haworth at the Smithsonian, Washington, D.C.

("Rick") West, the director of the Smithsonian's National Museum of the American Indian. John accompanied us to Rick's office, where we discussed our proposed Seth Eastman exhibition in New York and related events including children's programs. We needed Rick's approval and he gave it to us, with much enthusiasm. Rick is a member of the Cheyenne-Arapaho Tribes of Oklahoma and has a law degree from Stanford. The son of noted Indian artist Walter Richard West, Sr., he served as general counsel and special counsel to numerous Indian tribes and practiced law in Albuquerque before being appointed "founding director" of NMAI, which was established by an act of Congress in 1989.

John Haworth also took Paul and me to see NMAI's spectacular new Cultural Resources Center in Suitland, Maryland, six miles outside Washington, D.C. Native and non-Native researchers, scholars, and others from academic, cultural, and educational organizations come here to study Native American materials. NMAI collections were in the process of being moved from the museum's former Research Branch in the Bronx and catalogued when we were there. Once this work is complete, in four or five years' time, the Suitland facility will be the repository for several million artifacts from North and South America.

This Washington trip also provided

an unexpected opportunity that led to a gorgeous new book for Afton Press. A portion of the Ralph Rapson exhibition that originated in Minneapolis had traveled to The Octagon, where Paul and I went to see it. Dating to 1801, this brick, octagon-shaped house at 18th Street and New York Avenue N.W. was designed by William Thornton, the first architect of the U.S. Capitol, and was the first house in the area. During the War of 1812, it served as a temporary residence for James and Dolley Madison after the White House was burned. Now a national historic landmark, The Octagon is the oldest museum in the United States devoted to architecture and design.

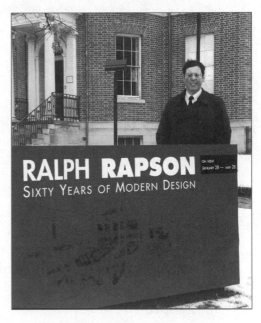

Paul Druckman at The Octagon

Octagon curator Linnea Hamer took us through the museum and gave us an order for more *Ralph Rapson* books, which were enjoying brisk sales in connection with the exhibition. At its small sales counter, along with the Rapson book, The Octagon was also selling copies of *Abandonings*, a book of color photographs of deteriorating farm buildings by architectural photographer Maxwell MacKenzie. A recent exhibition at The Octagon had featured MacKenzie's more recent black-and-white photographs along these same lines. We admired *Abandonings*—it was somewhat reminiscent of *Death of the Dream*—and in talking with Linnea, learned that she was related to MacKenzie. Her cousin Rebecca was married to him.

Reviewing plans for Seth Eastman exhibition with graphic designer Barbara Suhr and exhibits manager Peter Brill in New York

Linnea put us in touch with the MacKenzies, and they invited us to their home in Washington, D.C. Rebecca made lunch for us, and they showed us some of Max's gigantic ten-foot-long panoramic black-and-white photographs that were in between museum exhibitions—pictures of abandoned buildings set amidst vast, deserted prairies, enormous wheat fields, and huge, often glorious skies in North and South Dakota, Montana, Idaho, and Minnesota. We liked the photographs, we liked the MacKenzies, and we made plans with the MacKenzies to publish a book of these truly stunning photographs in 2001 titled *American Ruins: Ghosts on the Landscape.*

I did a fair amount of traveling for Afton Press in 2000. There were several trips to New York to plan the Seth Eastman exhibition and help make it happen. Paul Druckman and I met numerous times with John Haworth and members of his staff. We discussed everything from deciding who would write the copy for the text panels to accompany the paintings (Sarah Boehme and Christian Feest, my co-authors for *Seth Eastman: A Portfolio of North American Indians*) and how the watercolors should be framed, to how best to publicize the exhibition. We laid plans for the opening night gala and premiering

Paul Druckman and John Haworth in New York during planning session for Seth Eastman exhibition

the Eastman documentary in New York. We also helped develop children's programming to accompany the exhibition. In the evenings, we'd dine with John at one of his favorite places, or sometimes at Les Halles, a French restaurant that has become one of mine.

In March, for the first time, Afton exhibited books at the London International Book Fair (LIBF). Paul Druckman and I traveled to London to set up our display and staff it. This was quite a thrill for me, my first trip overseas since going to Scotland for Duncan MacMillan's *MacGhillemhaoil* book project in 1987, and we arrived a day early by design. Rick West had arranged for us to meet with British Museum curator Jonathan King, who gave us a private tour of the introductory display in the museum's new Chase Manhattan Gallery of North America: *First People, First Contact: Native Peoples of North America*. I'm always anxious for any opportunity to view Native American artifacts, and this exhibition was a particularly well-organized overview of Native American cultures.

We shared booth space at the London Book Fair with Jan Nathan, the executive director of Publishers Marketing Association (PMA), who was exhibiting member publisher's books. Jan also edits PMA's monthly publication, which always contains a wealth of helpful information for publishers. Paul and I worked hard at making the most of this London trade show and spent long hours on the floor, building Afton Press's reputation and contacts. We also had a chance to meet with European sales reps from Ingram Books, one of the wholesalers that represents us overseas. This show was a tremendous learning experience in international marketing, and we were able to observe which books sold and which ones didn't. Our most popular book with this mostly European audience was *Death of the Dream*.

We also met up with other publisher friends at LIBF.

With Jan Nathan and Afton books
at London International Book Fair

One evening Matt Hurley from *Publisher's Weekly* invited Paul and me to supper at an English pub with some of his colleagues from the magazine and a few other publishers. We had met Matt several months earlier when he was speaking at a Publishers Roundtable luncheon in St. Paul. Was this really me, drinking ale and eating steak with other publishers in jolly old England! One minute I couldn't believe my good fortune. But then the very next, I had a sorry jolt. I realized that I had broken the lower back molar on the right side of my mouth. I didn't know what happened to it—it was just missing—and the edge of what was left of my tooth was very sharp against my tongue.

I didn't mention my broken tooth to anyone that evening, it didn't hurt, but by the next morning the edge of my tongue was raw from rubbing against it. As the day wore on—it was Sunday and we were on the exhibition floor at the Book Fair all day—my tongue became so sore that it hurt to swallow anything, even water. Paul suggested I put some gum on my tooth to protect my tongue, and I found some across the street in a drugstore. He thought that the concierge at the hotel could probably locate a dentist for me that evening.

Looking back, I still find it amazing that the concierge *did* locate a dentist for me, on a Sunday evening, a woman who instructed me to meet her in an hour at her office, which was just a short distance from where we were staying in London at the Marriott at Marble Arch. In about twenty minutes time, this very capable dentist, who arrived at her office with her ten-year-old son in tow, put a temporary cap on my tooth. When I showed it to my dentist back home, he said that it looked pretty good. He suggested I call him when it cracked, and so far it hasn't.

The same day that we packed up our books in London, we flew to Paris in the evening to attend Salon du Livre the next day. Flying into Paris at night was like flying into an enchanted city: Paris was lit up like a circus. As the plane descended toward the airport, we could make out the dancing lights on the Eiffel Tower and the millennium ferris wheel. After hurrying through customs, we rented a car and drove down the Champs Élysées toward the Arc de Triomphe on the way to a small hotel, the Opera Cadet on rue Cadet. I could live at the Opera Cadet, for a long time.

My room and bath were lovely, vintage 1930s but with all the modern conveniences including a television (which I never watched) and an outlet for my electric curling iron (which I needed). Each morning, before setting off on the day's adventures, we ate breakfast ("le petit-déjeuner") in "la salle à manger," a ground floor dining room that opened onto a walled garden at the back of the hotel. Outside the Opera Cadet's front doors ran a narrow street that was lined each day with street vendors selling flowers, fruits and vegetables, pastries, and even grilled chickens. I bought yellow tulips for the small round table in the sitting area of my room.

Afton Press didn't exhibit at Salon du Livre. Instead we used this show to do more networking and to continue learning all that we could about new books and the international book market. Paul's wife, Jean Hardginski, joined us in Paris, and we also took a few days for sightseeing. Jean and Paul go to Paris several times each year—Paul is writing some guidebooks on Paris—but this was my first time in France.

At Nôtre Dame

Packing as many museums and historic sites as we could into each day, we visited the Rodin Museum, the Monet Museum, the Musée d'Orsay, and the Cluny Museum of the Middle Ages (which is built atop the ruins of Gallo-Roman baths dating to the first century). We dined at Bofingers, an "in" eatery for Parisians and famous people (including Meryl Streep, Madonna, Charlton Heston, and Steven Spielberg) and ate crepes that we purchased from street vendors. We heard Sunday Mass at Nôtre-Dame, and admired the stained glass windows at Sainte-Chapelle, the church built in the thirteenth century by Louis IX, the future St. Louis, to house the Relics of the Passion (now dispersed).

We also attended a cooking demonstration at the Ritz-Escoffier School of Gastronomy at the invitation of Chef Jean-Philippe Zahm and his assistant, Michelle Modem. We had met these two charming people a few months earlier when they were presenting a program and cooking demonstration at The Woman's Club in Minneapolis. The Woman's Club, in the Loring Park neighborhood, has twelve hundred members, including a handful of men, and periodically schedules Afton Historical Society Press authors for its afternoon programs.

I am frequently invited to the lunch that precedes the afternoon program, and I have met a lot of interesting people there. One time I was seated at lunch with Chris Jussel from *Antiques Roadshow*, who turned out to be every bit as nice as he appears on TV. Chris was the speaker that day, and I told him about my term paper with the Brooklyn Dodgers' signatures. He appeared to be genuinely interested, but he had taken a new job with Sotheby's and was no longer part of the television program. I am still waiting for an opportunity to appear on this show.

In Paris, the cooking demonstration Jean and Paul and I sat in on was held in the basement level of the Ritz hotel for an audience of about thirty people, most of them well-dressed women. When it was over, we were approached by a man who noticed the Afton Historical Society Press tote bags we all three were carrying and introduced himself. Were we really from the Afton Press, he wanted to know. He was one of our fans and customers and particularly enjoyed our Mabel Seeley novels!

Refreshed by our brief holiday in Paris, I arrived back in Minnesota in time to take

With Paul and Jean and our Afton tote bags in Paris

delivery of our first book for 2000, *Small Town Minnesota: A to Z*, by first-time author Tony Andersen, which would turn out to be our best-selling book of the year. That *Small Town* sold so well came as a very pleasant surprise. When Tony had first called me and described this book about a year earlier, I hadn't been able to get very excited about it. The "A to Z" part sounded silly to me. But Tony had already taken thousands of photographs for his proposed book and written text for it, so I agreed to take a look at it.

I'm glad I did. I was struck by the simple beauty of the photographs Tony showed me. They were honest and forthright and full of good humor. The text he wrote to accompany them was equally refreshing. Tony's approach to small towns reminded me a little of the road trip that author William Least Heat Moon chronicled a few years ago in *Blue Highways*. Lugging a bunch of camera gear that included a stepladder, Tony had gone about photographing twenty-six randomly selected Minnesota towns, one for each letter of

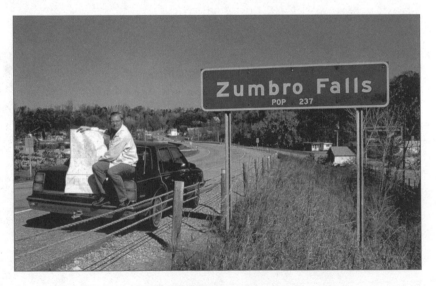

Tony Andersen on the road

the alphabet. His simple criteria required that these towns have less than one thousand residents and be distributed fairly evenly throughout the state.

Author Bill Holm, who befriended Tony during his odyssey, wrote in the Foreword to *Small Town*: "Tony Andersen arrived in this alphabet of towns armed not only with his camera, but with love, curiosity, humor, and a good eye. I commend his vision to you." Brian Lambert of the *St. Paul Pioneer Press* noted that the book was about "real people of real towns" that are some "of the last corners of America left untouched by Starbucks, the Gap and ramp meters." Al Mathieson in the *Fillmore County Journal* called the book "heartfelt and eloquent."

During the summer, books in hand and for sale, Tony revisited many of the towns he had written about, attending celebrations, carnivals, and parades. Sometimes he drove to these places in the 1989 Oldsmobile Delta 88 he had purchased to travel throughout Minnesota to take his photographs. At other times his father piloted him in the senior Andersen's private plane. We called attention to "Tony's Tour" on our website, where we posted a gallery of Tony's photographs from *Small Town Minnesota*.

Small Town Minnesota was a joy to produce and market, a project that went smoothly from day one. Most of our book projects proceed pretty much this way. There is, on occasion, however, the exception. When it came time for our second year 2000 book to arrive from the printer in April, it didn't. This was Jon Hassler's *Rufus at the Door & Other Stories*, which we finally concluded had a hex on it. Friesens ended up printing it four times to get it right. Like Jon's earlier book for us, *Keepsakes & Other Stories*, *Rufus* is illustrated with two-color wood engravings by Gaylord Schanilec. The first time Friesens printed *Rufus*, it omitted the second, smokey blue, color. It was at least partly my fault that this book got printed that way.

Rufus was already behind schedule, and I was worried that it wouldn't arrive in time for a party we had scheduled for Jon Hassler in May, when our account rep, Tim Fast, called me from Canada. He was sending press proofs by FedEx to arrive the next day, Saturday, he said. If he didn't hear from me by Sunday evening, he was going to go ahead and print and bind this book to make sure that we had books when we needed them.

Saturday came and I didn't receive any press proofs. I would learn later that the FedEx driver had attempted to deliver them to the coffee shop that rented space in our building, but the coffee shop woman refused to accept them, and they were returned to Friesens. Had I seen them, I would have called Tim immediately to say, "Hold the presses." Instead, when I didn't receive them, I decided to say nothing and let the printing proceed. Friesens had never let us down. They always did beautiful work. Why should now be any different? If this job were held up any longer, we wouldn't have books for Jon's party.

We almost went into shock a week later when we received the first advance copies of *Rufus* with its illustrations printed in black ink only. The entire printing, five thousand hardcover books, had to be shredded. Then the second and third times Friesens printed *Rufus*, a glitch in the binding process created small tears on the front pages of each book. Things were getting so bad they were almost, but not *really*, funny; this book was jinxed. Friesens absorbed all of the reprinting and binding costs for *Rufus*, but we didn't have books until well into summer, which meant that we missed anticipated Mother's Day and Father's Day sales.

In the meantime, we went ahead with the extravagant

Desserts table at
"Celebrating Jon Hassler"

publication party we had planned for Jon Hassler and *Rufus* at The Woman's Club on May 21. Earlier in the year Jon had told us that he wouldn't be able to make public appearances in 2000 for health reasons, but he had agreed to this one grand party that we were calling "Celebrating Jon Hassler." It was more than a publication party, it was a well-staged event to recognize Jon's lifetime accomplishments. In April, at the annual Minnesota Book Awards ceremony at the Minnesota History Center in St. Paul, Jon had received the prestigious Flanagan Prize for excellence and achievement in the literature and culture of the Midwest.

For "Celebrating Jon Hassler," we put together an hour-long program of tributes from Jon's friends and admirers in the auditorium at The Woman's Club and afterwards served exquisite desserts and coffee in the main-floor dining room and lounge. We had all of our Afton Press books on display, and we also had a long table filled with copies of all of Jon's books in their various formats: hardcover, softcover, large print, and foreign language editions. Friesens was able to send us a hundred or so softcover copies of *Rufus* (they arrived that same day by air), which Jon signed at home before the party. When these quickly sold out, we took orders and later mailed the books to customers.

Several years ago, Jon Hassler was diagnosed with Parkinson's disease. His 1999 holiday letter to his friends (which we included in *Rufus at the Door*) was from Agatha McGee, his most enduring character, who explained about Jon's Parkinson's and how he was coping with it.

> Dr. Parkinson [Agatha wrote], having lived with my friend for the past six years, has begun to behave in cruel and irritating ways. He has rendered the novelist's handwriting illegible, has caused him to fall down a number of times (the current number being 93), and has lowered his voice to the point where it's hard to understand.
>
> "He's quite a practical joker," my friend says of the despicable doctor. "I've been giving quite a few public readings this season, and I find myself at a disadvantage, because I'm gradually losing my ability to perform the three tasks necessary for a reading; namely, walking up to the podium, reading aloud, and autographing."

I myself had seen Jon fall down on more than one occasion. When Paul Druckman and I were in New York at the same time as the Hasslers the previous November, we told Jon and Gretchen that we would pick them up one evening at their hotel for dinner and to see the Broadway show *Cats*. That would be fine, Jon said. They would be outside waiting for us. When we drove up, Jon took a halting step towards our car and fell onto the pavement, cutting his lip and hand. We helped him into the back seat of the car and he wiped himself off with his handkerchief and that was the end of it. He didn't complain. Somehow Jon has learned to

With Jon and Gretchen Hassler

fall without seriously hurting himself. "I freeze starting out," he told us, "but once I'm on my way I'm fine. It's the first two or three steps that cause me to stumble."

We also had a fourth Mabel Seeley title on our spring 2000 list. *The Crying Sisters* arrived from Friesens in June without a hitch, making both us and our growing cadre of Mabel Seeley fans happy. An immediate success when it was first published in New York in 1939, *The Crying Sisters* is about Janet Ruell, a small-town librarian on vacation who goes looking for adventure. Jilted eight years earlier and still single at twenty-nine, she is running away from a proposal from an unambitious forty-year-old bank cashier named George Train. Janet, of course, finds adventure in spades in this well-crafted mystery with a double plot. Does she also find romance? I'll only say that Mabel Seeley's stories do not disappoint.

Barb Arney designed *Small Town Minnesota*, and Mary Sue designed *Rufus at the Door* and *The Crying Sisters*. By summer Mary Sue was also designing two more books for us, *Painting the Dakota: Seth Eastman at Fort Snelling* by award-winning children's book author Marybeth Lorbiecki, and our holiday book, *Christmas on West Seventh Street*, by cartoonist Jerry Fearing. One Sunday when Mary Sue was on tour and performing at Country Jam U.S.A. in Eau Claire, Wisconsin, about an hour away from us, Charlie and I drove there to see her. I took along her page proofs for *Christmas on West Seventh Street*, on which I had marked corrections, and Mary Sue made the changes on her laptop computer between shows.

I was also working on a book of my own, this one, *Pie in the Sky*. I had been working on it off and on for a couple of years, but now we had it on our year 2001 list. I needed some time away from the office to devote to it, so in late

June, with spring projects behind us and the flurry of fall still ahead of us, Charlie and I retreated to Utah, where we have a small house in the mountain town of Helper. Charlie is always ready to go to Utah. He likes poking around, searching out signs of early Indian life in this high desert country, an area rich in pre-historic rock art, petroglyphs and pictographs. The year before, underneath a rock overhang, he had located a granary cist from an ancient culture.

Helper is a depressed coal-mining and railroad town, two hours south of Salt Lake. It's called Helper because this is where they put the "helper" engines on the coal trains to help them over the mountains to Salt Lake. Our daughter Patty was raising her two young sons in Helper when we purchased our house there several years ago. She has since moved to Eugene, Oregon, where she is heading up a wetlands conservation project and building an environmental center. Patty refurbished several historic houses and commercial buildings in Helper, including two downtown brick buildings on Main Street in which she opened a coffee shop and an art gallery. She also turned a former coal company house into a comfortable haven for Charlie and me.

Our house is one of many small houses that had been built in the mountains for miners which were later moved into Helper. It had

Patty with her sons, Damon and Dylan, in Oregon

232

been empty for ten years when we bought it. Patty gutted it, saving only the wide floor boards and some interior woodwork, and put it back together for us. She did a lot of the work herself and hired workmen to do what she couldn't or didn't have time to do—the sheetrocking, painting, and tile work in the kitchen and bathroom. On several trips to the desert, she and Charlie collected the red rock that the tile man used to face the fireplace in the living room. Charlie calls this place "Lonesome Dove," and hung up an autographed publicity photo of Robert Duvall ("Gus" in the film *Lonesome Dove*) inside the front door.

Our "Lonesome Dove" house in Helper, Utah

It's an easy house to come to for two weeks at a time, which is what we usually do, two or three times a year. It's small enough—just four rooms and a bath—that it doesn't require much housekeeping, and with no outside pressures of any kind, we can unwind and work or relax as we please. Except in wet weather, which is rare in Helper, I'm up each morning at dawn and out hiking with our dog, Cody, on the abandoned railroad grade that runs along the base of the mountains behind our

Charlie and our dog Cody on the porch of "Lonesome Dove"

house. This is my favorite time of the day. The gorgeous red-rock scenery is the stuff of old Westerns and reminds me of the Roy Rogers and Gene Autry matinees that I was so enamored with as a very young girl.

During the summer of 2000 I had my laptop and a small printer with me in Helper and worked part of every day at the kitchen table, roughing out the last five chapters of *Pie in the Sky*. Most afternoons Charlie and I would take drives, to the desert, to neighboring towns, to high mountain places where Charlie fished. On the Fourth of July, which is a quiet day in Helper, with no parade, I took a picture of a Statue of Liberty that one of our neighbors had erected in his front yard. The year before I had been in New York and saw the Statue of Liberty in person on Independence Day, and I have ever since had special feelings for this special lady.

Back in 1995, when Afton published *Seth Eastman: A Portfolio of North American Indians* and a companion volume by Eastman's wife, Mary Henderson Eastman, *Dahcotah; or, Life and Legends of the Sioux*, we surely felt that we had done all that we ever would or could do on the subject of Seth Eastman. But no. Afton was revisiting Seth Eastman in 2000. We actually had three new Seth Eastman projects in progress, each of which complemented and enhanced the others.

In September we published our first book for young people, *Painting the Dakota: Seth Eastman at Fort Snelling*, illustrated with drawings and paintings by Seth Eastman. We launched this book with a media event at historic Fort

Press check for Painting the Dakota
*at Friesens' state-of-the-art printing plant
in Altona, Canada*

Snelling, where Eastman had been an officer in the 1840s. We also used this occasion to announce the public television documentary based on our Eastman books that we were co-producing with Twin Cities Public Television (TPT, formerly known as KTCA-TV), as well our exhibition of the MacMillan Collection of Seth Eastman watercolors at the Smithsonian's National Museum of the American Indian in New York in April 2001.

The impressive afternoon program we put together at Fort Snelling for local television and newspaper people included remarks by TPT President Jim Pagliarini, independent producer Kristian Berg (who was writing and directing the Seth Eastman documentary), Minneapolis Institute of Arts Director Evan Maurer, author Christian F. Feest (*Seth Eastman: A Portfolio of North American Indians*), and John Haworth from New York. Christian Feest, who joined us from Germany, also came to Afton the following day where we discussed his next project for Afton Press, a book about artist Frank Mayer, who traveled from Baltimore to Minnesota in 1851 to paint the native Indians.

Our goal now is to place copies of *Painting the Dakota: Seth Eastman at Fort Snelling* in classrooms throughout Minnesota. Our Friends of the Afton Historical Society Press are helping us to do so. In August, Louise Klas, who organized the Friends group, held a garden party in our back yard at the Afton Press that raised almost $3,000 for this program. Louise is a former English teacher, lawyer, civic volunteer, and also the mother of my assistant, Annie Klas. Thirty-five new members joined the Friends at the garden party, which we all considered a great success. Louise is an absolute angel to help us in the many ways that she does.

We are also seeking and receiving contributions from additional sources to help us provide books for schools. The Andersen Foundation in Bayport, Minnesota, gave us a generous donation to place copies of *Painting the Dakota* in St. Croix Valley area schools. Former Minnesota Governor Elmer L. Andersen, whom I have known and admired for many years, is another terrific supporter for our projects.

In August I visited Governor Andersen at his spacious home in the St. Paul suburb of Arden Hills. A young woman assistant greeted me at the door and showed me in. Elmer was waiting for me in his library, seated at one end of the large table in the middle of the room with his back to the door. I went up to him, kissed him hello on the cheek, and sat down on his right. There was a tray with a carafe of coffee, cream, sugar, and cookies on the table, so I poured coffee for both of us.

Governor Andersen was ninety and suffering from post-polio syndrome that confined him to a wheelchair, but his health and spirits were good and his mind clear. He knew what I had come for. I had written to him, asking for help with two of our projects: the *Painting the Dakota* books for schools program, and also funding for a new book, *Ojibwe: We Look in All Directions*. This second book, by Ojibwe scholar Thomas Peacock, is a history of the Ojibwe nation, a companion volume to a six-part public television documentary that WDSE-TV was producing in Duluth.

Elmer was eager to hear more about both of these book projects and told me that he and his wife Eleanor would support them personally. He also told me how to apply to the Elmer L. and Eleanor J. Andersen Foundation for additional monies. The next week I received a letter from Governor Andersen stating that he and Eleanor were giving the Afton Press a gift of H. B. Fuller Company stock. H. B. Fuller is an adhesives company that Andersen turned into a world leader.

Our final book in 2000 was *Christmas on West Seventh*

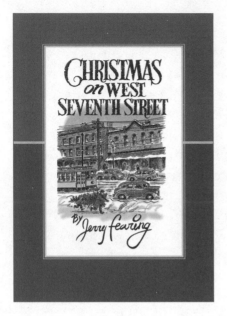

Street by Jerry Fearing, a nostalgic look back in text and cartoons to a simpler, more innocent time. The year is 1940. The country had just passed through the Depression, and the war in Europe was still half a world away. Fearing's generation of children didn't have television or computer games. Instead they enjoyed radio, great movies, and terrific comic strips. "Then as now," wrote Fearing, "the religious significance of Christ's birthday was the last thing on a kid's mind. It was the colorful trappings, the Santa legend, and *GIFTS* that captured and held our attention. Christmas was the most exciting day of the year in a kid's life."

Jerry Fearing was staff artist and cartoonist for the *St. Paul Pioneer Press* for more than forty years. In the 1970s his syndicated comic strip, *Rooftop O'Toole*, ran in eighty papers across the country. Rooftop was a newsboy who delivered papers to the White House, and the strip dealt with political issues beginning in the Ford administration. "It was a relaxed, informal time in Washington, and Ford was an interesting and funny guy," says Fearing. Things got even better after Jimmy Carter was elected. Who could fail to appreciate characters like Miss Lillian, Billy, Amy, and the Carters' dog Grits.

Jerry signed copies of *Christmas on West Seventh Street* at the Upper Midwest Booksellers Association (UMBA) conference in St. Paul in September, adding a small cartoon to each signature, and went on to sign books for customers at numerous stores and locations right up until Christmas. He was invited to The Woman's Club in Minneapolis, where he presented an afternoon program about his new book and his overall career, and he was the featured author at our Afton Christmas party for friends and customers at Landmark Center on December 8.

Christmas on West Seventh Street proved every bit as popular as we had thought it would be, and by December we had also scheduled our year 2001 Christmas book, by former Minnesota Senator Eugene McCarthy. McCarthy, who now lives in Washington, D.C., is a friend of Louise Klas and her husband, Bill, and stays with them on his frequent trips to St. Paul (in their house designed by architect Clarence Johnston in the Crocus Hill neighborhood). I had told Louise that I would like to meet McCarthy, and she and Bill brought him to my office during the summer. At eighty-four, McCarthy is an important American writer and a terrific wit who regaled us with political and Catholic stories. Much to my delight, he said yes to our proposal that he write a book for Afton Press. I asked him to think about including "some good Catholic stuff."

A distinguished (and still terrifically handsome) senior statesman, Eugene McCarthy was elected to Congress from Minnesota in 1948 and served five terms in the House and two in the Senate. In 1968 he became enormously popular with much of America's youth by forming a "coalition of conscience" against the war in Vietnam. At the time of the Democratic convention in Chicago that nominated Hubert Humphrey for president in 1968, McCarthy was leading Republican contender Richard Nixon in the national polls, and he ran again for president, as an independent, in 1976 and 1992.

The day the Klases brought McCarthy to Afton, we ate lunch at The Dock restaurant, which overlooks the St. Croix River in Stillwater. The Dock is an exceptional glass and timbers building designed by Stillwater architect Mike McGuire, the same Mike McGuire who in 1976 designed my terrific office space, overlooking the same St. Croix River. In 2000, after purchasing the entire building in Afton in which the Afton Press was renting space, we hired Mike to renovate it.

Things have happened pretty fast for the Afton Press. We were just six years old in 2000, and I find a lot of what we're doing hard to believe myself. We're accomplishing some terrifically good things of which we are justifiably proud. This includes bringing the Seth Eastman paintings of Dakota Indian life to a wide national and international audience. These paintings are particularly important to the Dakota people themselves. Dakota leaders have told us that Seth Eastman's work has given them a richer understanding of their traditional life and the ways of their people.

The Shakopee Mdewakanton Dakota Community in Prior Lake, Minnesota, commissioned stained glass windows based on the Eastman paintings for its new spiritual center, Tiowakan (Dakota for "Spirit Within"). This community, which includes descendants of Seth Eastman and his Dakota wife, Wakaninajinwin (Stands Sacred), also helped fund the Seth Eastman documentary co-produced by Twin Cities Public Television and Afton Historical Society Press.

Bill Gabler's *Death of the Dream* is another terrific success story. Bill had been turned down by other publishers before he came to us with his haunting photographs of dilapidated farmsteads—the homes of our pioneer ancestors that are rapidly disappearing from the Midwestern prairies. Producer John Whitehead and Twin Cities Public Television found the stories to go along with the pictures, told by people who had lived the "the Dream" of life on the farm, and together TPT and Afton produced the enormously popular video, *Death of the Dream: Farmhouses in the Heartland*. During 2000 *Death of the Dream* was seen by hundreds of thousands of viewers across the country and generated a half million dollars in revenue for PBS stations that used it for pledge drives.

We've had some very good luck, and we are also blessed with incredibly talented, versatile, and dedicated staff. Our office runs very efficiently with the help of my assistants, Sue Andraschko and Annie Klas, and our bookkeeper, Cora Dorsey.

Our marketing director Paul Druckman keeps pointing us in new and exciting directions, including new documentaries and new museum exhibitions. My daughter Mary Sue continues to design beautiful books (including *Pie in the Sky*) for us. My son, Chuck Johnston, who began by designing our website, is now our development officer.

Steve Anderson still helps us with shipping (although most of the rest of us also take turns now and then at delivering books to Bookmen and Twin Cities stores, especially in the hectic few weeks just before Christmas). We also work with free-lance editors and designers, especially editor Phil Freshman and designer Barb Arney. A loyal cadre of volunteers, led by Afton author Ed Robb and local residents Madelyn Green and Pat Schultz, helps us with special projects and mailings.

It is because of the generous spirit of all of these people that the Afton Press is enjoying such enormous success, and I am grateful to each of them.

We began this incredibly lucky (for us) Year of the Dragon by winning the Publisher of the Year Award presented by the Midwest Independent Publishers Association (MIPA). We also won MIPA Awards for *Peoples of the Twilight: European Views of Minnesota, 1823-1865; Ralph Rapson: Sixty Years of Modern Design* (which also won the 2000 David Stanley Gebhard Award and the 2000 Independent Publishers Magazine Award); and *Keepsakes & Other Stories*; as well as for our catalog. In May, Jon Hassler's *Keepsakes* won the Publishers Marketing Association's Benjamin Franklin Award for Best Cover Design. I accepted in Chicago on

Four Emmys! Joe Demko, John Whitehead, Patricia Johnston, Paul Druckman, Robert Hutchins, and Steven Heitzeg

behalf of Mary Sue who was on tour with her band.

On the evening of October 21, 2000, we attended our first Emmy Awards ceremony, at the University of Minnesota. Everybody who was anybody in the Twin Cities television community was there, and we enjoyed great food and wine and lots of interesting conversation. When it was all said and done, our documentary with TPT, *Death of the Dream*, had won four Emmys—for best writing (John Whitehead), best audio (Joe Demko), best videography (Robert Hutchins), and best musical score (Steven Heitzeg).

Death of the Dream won more Emmys than any other program that evening, and these guys really deserved them. They had put their hearts and souls into this production, which will continue to attract wide audiences for many years to come.

Six years ago I could not have foreseen the high excitement and immense satisfaction that the Afton Press is experiencing today. Twenty-some years ago I could not have foreseen that an article about Cream of Wheat ads would one day lead to the Afton Historical Society Press. The bottom line is that writing and publishing have been very good to me and for me. It's a good life and for more I could not ask.

When I turned on my laptop this morning, the day I finished this final chapter of *Pie in the Sky*, this message came up on my screen:

> *If you do your best,*
> *whatever happens will*
> *be for the best.*

It was the computer program's helpful tip for the day, and a fitting final bit of advice, supplied by a machine, but my sentiments exactly.

1994

Johnston, Patricia Condon. *The Shape of Things: The Art of Francis Lee Jaques*, 11"x 11", 168 pp., 100 color plus b/w illustrations, bibliography, hardcover (linen) with dustjacket (see pages 106, 149–150, 155, 157, 166-167)

1995 Minnesota Book Award
1995 Midwest Independent Publishers Award

1995

Boehme, Sarah E., Christian F. Feest, and Patricia Condon Johnston. *Seth Eastman: A Portfolio of North American Indians*, 12" x 12", 196 pp., 100 illustrations, 85 in color including 56 color plates, notes, hardcover (linen) with dustjacket (see pages 154, 169–174, 190-191, 198, 199, 220, 234, 235)

Certificate of Recognition,
1996 Northeastern Minnesota Book Awards

Eastman, Mary Henderson. *Dahcotah; or, Life and Legends of the Sioux*, 7 1/2" x 9 1/2", 240 pp., 20 color illustrations, hardcover (linen) with dustjacket (see pages 154, 172, 173, 199, 234)

Johnston, Patricia Condon. *Stillwater: Minnesota's Birthplace in Photographs by John Runk*, 8 1/2" x 10 1/4", 104 pp., 80 duotone photographs, bibliography, index (see pages xi, 3, 85–96, 101, 154)

Price, Susan Davis. *Minnesota Gardens: An Illustrated History*, 10" x 10 1/4", 168 pp., 100 color and duotone photos, notes, bibliography, index, hardcover (linen) with dustjacket (see pages 153–154, 168, 172–173)

1997 Best of Show Award, Midwest Independent Publishers Association
1997 Midwest Independent Publishers Award
1996 Minnesota Book Award
1996 Quill and Trowel Award, Garden Writers Association

1996

Coen, Rena Neumann. *Minnesota Impressionists*, 10" X 10 1/8", 96 pp., 43 color plates, reading list, hardcover (linen) with dustjacket (see pages 175–178)

Certificate of Recognition,
1997 Northeastern Minnesota Book Awards
1997 Midwest Independent Publishers Award

Heilbron, Bertha. *Christmas and New Year's on the Minnesota Frontier*, 9" x 6", 64 pp., hardcover (see page 184)

Larson, Paul Clifford. *Minnesota Architect: The Life and Work of Clarence H. Johnston*, 10½" x 12", 224 pp., 280 photos and illustrations, notes, appendices, bibliography, index, hardcover (linen) with dustjacket (see pages 180–183, 191, 199)

1997 David Stanley Gebhard Award
1997 Minnesota Book Award
1997 Midwest Independent Publishers Award

Robb, Edwin G. *Afton Remembered*, 8½" x 8", 120 pp., 86 photos, bibliography, index, hardcover (linen) with dustjacket (see pages 178–180, 240)

1997

Gabler, William G. *Death of the Dream: Classic Minnesota Farmhouses*, 10¼" x 11½", 128 pp., 87 illustrations including 72 tritone plates, reading list, hardcover (linen) with dustjacket, reprinted in softcover in 1999 as *Death of the Dream: Farmhouses in the Heartland* (see pages 188–189, 191, 194, 199)

Holm, Bill. *Faces of Christmas Past*, 9" x 6", 64 pp., hardcover with dustjacket (see pages 185–186, 214)

Koop, Steven E., M.D. *We Hold This Treasure*, 11" x 9¼", 192 pp., 175 duotone photos and illustrations, notes, appendices, index, hardcover (linen) with dustjacket

1998 Midwest Independent Publishers Award

Larson, Paul Clifford. *Icy Pleasures*, 10¼" x 10¼", 168 pp., 160 color and mechanically colored duotone photos, hardcover (linen) with dustjacket (see pages 183, 199)

1998 Midwest Independent Publishers Award
1998 Midwest Book Award

1998

Feest, Christian F., and Sylvia S. Kasprycki. *Peoples of the Twilight: European Views of Native Minnesota, 1823–1865*, 10½" x 8¼", 316 pp., 97 illustrations, annotated catalog of illustrations, hardcover in slipcase, also handbound signed and numbered edition in slipcase (see pages 170, 198–199)

1999 Midwest Independent Publishers Award

Hassler, Jon. *Underground Christmas*, 9" x 6", 64 pp., hardcover with dustjacket, also handbound signed and numbered edition in slipcase (see pages 186–187)

Larson, Paul Clifford. *A Place at the Lake*, 9¾" x 11½", 160 pp., 140 full color and tinted photos, hardcover (linen) with dustjacket (see pages 183–184, 195–196, 197, 199)

1999 Independent Publishers Magazine Award

MacMillan, Duncan W. *MacMillan: The American Grain Family*, 10¼" x 8⅝", 350 pp., 325 photos, hardcover (linen) with dustjacket (see pages 117, 123, 125–141, 148–149, 181, 195, 196–197)

1998 Midwest Independent Publishers Award
1999 Independent Publishers Magazine Award

Seeley, Mabel. *The Beckoning Door*, 9½" x 6¼", 226 pp., hardcover with dustjacket (see page 203)

Seeley, Mabel. *The Chuckling Fingers*, 9½" x 6¼", 312 pp., hardcover with dustjacket (see pages 200–201)

1999

Bly, Carol. *An Adolescent's Christmas: 1944*, 9" x 6", 64 pp., hardcover with dustjacket, also handbound signed and numbered edition in slipcase (see pages 211–212, 214)

Hassler, Jon. *Keepsakes & Other Stories*, 10" x 7¼", 120 pp., hardcover with dustjacket, also softcover, also handbound signed and numbered edition in slipcase (see pages 187–188, 203, 211, 212, 214 227, 240)

1999 Midwest Independent Publishers Merit Award
2000 Benjamin Franklin Award

Hession, Jane King, Rip Rapson, and Bruce N. Wright. *Ralph Rapson: Sixty Years of Modern Design*, 11" x 10 1/2" 256 pp., 300 drawings and illustrations, notes, bibliography, index, hardcover with dustjacket, also handbound signed and numbered edition in slipcase (see pages 203–207, 211, 219, 240)

1999 Midwest Independent Publishers Award
2000 David Stanley Gebhard Award
2000 Independent Publishers Book Award

Seeley, Mabel. *The Whistling Shadow*, 9 1/2" x 6 1/4", 216 pp., hardcover with dustjacket (see pages 201–202, 210)

2000

Andersen, Tony. *Small Town Minnesota A to Z*, 8 1/4" x 10 1/4", 120 pp., 160 color photographs, softcover (see pages 213, 224–225, 229)

Fearing, Jerry. *Christmas on West Seventh Street*, 9" x 6", 64 pp., 30 cartoons, hardcover with dustjacket (see pages 229, 234–236)

Hassler, Jon. *Rufus at the Door & Other Stories*, 10" x 7 1/4", 128 pp., hardcover with dustjacket, also softcover, also handbound signed and numbered edition in slipcase (see pages 210, 213, 226-229)

Lorbiecki, Marybeth. *Painting the Dakota: Seth Eastman at Fort Snelling*, 9" x 10", 104 pp., 50 color illustrations, bibliography, index, softcover (see pages 174, 229, 232–234)

Seeley, Mabel. *The Crying Sisters*, 9 1/2" x 6 1/4", 328 pp., hardcover with dustjacket (see pages 201, 213, 228–229)

– Afton Historical Society Press –
2000 Midwest Independent Publishers Award:
Publisher of the Year

– Public Television Documentary –
Death of the Dream: Farmhouses in the Heartland, video running time 60 minutes (see pages 191–194, 209, 238)

Four 2000 Emmy Awards,
for Best Writing, Best Videography,
Best Audio, Best Musical Composition

Photo and Illustration Credits

THE CONDON FAMILY PHOTOGRAPHS that enliven this book were sent to me by my mother, Betty Condon, who lives in Hollywood, Florida. The Cream of Wheat ads, photo of Philip R. Goodwin, Roland Reed photos, and Gustaf Nordenskiold photos are from my personal collections. The MacMillan family photos and the Seth Eastman images are used courtesy of W. Duncan MacMillan. My thanks also to the following individuals and organizations who provided photographs and artwork:

Frontispiece: Emmy photo by Paul J. Druckman
2. Photo by Charles J. Johnston
22. Photo by Charles J. Johnston
50. Celtic Moon Publishing, Inc., Camp Hill, Pennsylvania
57. Minnesota Historical Society (MHS)
60. MHS
61. MHS, photo by Truman W. Ingersoll
62. MHS, photo by Truman W. Ingersoll
63. MHS
64. MHS
70. MHS, *Frances Densmore & American Indian Music*, Vol. XXIII of contributions from the Museum of the American Indian–Heye Foundation, page 131, plate 6
72. MHS
73. MHS
75. MHS
81. Stark Museum of Art, Orange, Texas
86. MHS, photo by John Runk
87. MHS, photo by John Runk
88. MHS, photo by John Runk
89. MHS, photos by John Runk
91. MHS, photo by John Runk
93. MHS, photo by John Runk
95. Photo by Charles J. Johnston
96. St. Louis County Historical Society
101. MHS
105. Photo by Charles J. Johnston

117. Photo by Charles J. Johnston
118. Hood Museum of Art, Dartmouth College,
Hanover, New Hampshire; gift of the Class of 1887
120. Sophia Smith Collection, Smith College
121. Sophia Smith Collection, Smith College
129. Photo by Charles J. Johnston
130. Photo by Charles J. Johnston
142. American Museum of Natural History Library
144. James Ford Bell Museum of Natural History,
University of Minnesota
165. Photo by O'Ann Christiansen
175. MHS
176. MHS
179. Afton Historical Society
181. MHS
186. Photo by Paul J. Druckman
189. Photos by William G. Gabler
193. Photo by Michael Trosman
197. Photo by Paul J. Druckman
204. Ralph Rapson
205. Photo by Paul J. Druckman
206. Photo by Paul J. Druckman
207. Photo by Paul J. Druckman
208. Photo by Paul J. Druckman
209. Photo by Paul J. Druckman
213. Photo by Paul J. Druckman
218. Photos by Paul J. Druckman
222. Photo by Paul J. Druckman
224. Photo by Paul J. Druckman
226. Photo by Tony Andersen
229. Photo by Paul J. Druckman
232. Photo by Chuck Johnston
235. Photo by Paul J. Druckman
241. Photo by Jean Hardginski

Designed by
Mary Susan Oleson
Afton, Minnesota, and Nashville, Tennessee

Typefaces are
Palatino and Lucida